Adventure Bound

Adventure Bound:

A Father and Daughter Circumnavigate the Greatest Lake in the World

By CARL BEHREND

Acknowledgements

I would first like to thank my parents, grandparents and great grandparents for choosing to live along the shores of the Great Lakes and for raising me in such a rich and beautiful environment.
This book is a result of those choices.
I would also like to thank my children Caleb, Sarah and Naomi for accompanying me on so many of my adventures.
I would also like to acknowledge all the authors and publishers of articles, books and periodicals that bring to life the stories of the Great Lakes, and the many people who have shared so many wonderful stories about our great and wonderful Lake Superior.
Finally, I would especially like to acknowledge my daughter, Naomi, for accompanying me on this voyage and for allowing me to share some of the notes from her diary. Even though she only logged part of the journey, I chose to include these passages in order to share her thoughts.

Old Country Books & Records
E7099 Maple Grove Road
Munising, MI 49862
906-387-2331
www.greatlakeslegends.com

Printed by: Malloy, Inc., Ann Arbor, MI
Cover Design: Tom O'Connell/Boomerang Marketing, Chatham, MI
Typesetting: Calumet Mac Services, Whiting, IN

Table of Contents

CHAPTER 1
THE SPARK

Robert Frost wrote:

Two roads diverged in a yellow wood,
And sorry I could not travel both
And be one traveler, long I stood
And looked down one as far as I could
Two where it bent in the undergrowth;

Then took the other, as just as fair
And having perhaps the better claim,
Because it was grassy and wanted wear
Though as for that the passing there
Had worn them really about the same

And both that morning equally lay
In leaves no step had trodden black,
Oh, I kept the first for another day!
Yet knowing how way leads on to way,
I doubted if I should ever come back

I shall be telling this with a sigh
Somewhere ages and ages hence:
Two roads diverged in a wood and I –
I took the road less traveled by,
And that has made all the difference.

A story cannot be told without a beginning.

I guess you could say this story began with a high school friend named Steve Johnson. He had a dream that was sparked by another sailing adventure: the voyage of the *Dove*. In that story, a teenage boy sets out on a journey around the world. On his way, the boy becomes a young man. He also meets his true love. When the journey is done the two lovers sail off into the sunset to enjoy a tropical paradise. That's all it took. That story sparked a fire—a fire that would burn for years to come—not only in Steve's life, but also in the lives of many of those around him.

Steve was a picture of the youth from the hippie days of the late 1960s and early 1970s. His long blonde hair, laid back lifestyle as an artist and sign painter and his seeming lack of motivation to strike out on his own made his family and friends wonder if his childhood would last indefinitely.

But along with that laid back attitude, Steve also had a certain charm and talent. In both his artwork and his sign painting, he showed a remarkable genius that often made you overlook his weaker attributes. One would look with wonder at his latest creation, whether it was sculpture, painting or billboard. With that same artistry and style, Steve set out to build his first sailboat.

He made the new sailboat from an old wooden rowboat. Steve made a mast from two-by-fours, which were carefully shaped to not only be useful, but also attractive. He also added artistic touches to the rest of the boat. The wooden rudder, the bow and the sail boom all had his signature of craftsmanship. For the crowning work, he named the boat the *Christine Louise*, after his girlfriend, Chris Burnis. The boat's name was painted in Steve's own unique style of lettering that I'm sure charmed Chris to no end. Together, the couple would sail the waters of Indian Lake, the lake where Steve's parents raised him.

This first boat of Steve's marked the beginning of a long line of sailboat ownership that would stretch into the next millennium. And with Steve's acquiring additional boats, others would follow his passion. The dream of one hopeless romantic is often contagious. Steve's cousin Kevin would be one of those who would follow the dream and the spark. In pursuing his own *"Dove"* vision, Steve's passion for bigger waves and bigger water meant getting a bigger boat.

Soon Steve, with the help of cousin Kevin, would be working on another boat: the *Clair Bastian*. Well, maybe it wasn't exactly his next boat. Actually, the next boat was the *Christine Louise II*, followed by *Christine Louise III* and then, the *Clair Bastian*. Steve and Kevin went in together on the purchase of the 26-foot Thunderbird sailboat. They bought the boat for $2,000 from a state police trooper who lived in Munising. The happy pair took the boat 45 miles south to Manistique to prepare it for their dream voyage.

Together, Steve and Kevin were able to restore the old sailboat and give her a whole new look. After about a year of preparation, the two were ready. Their plan was to sail from Manistique, Michigan south through

Lake Michigan to Chicago and then through various waterways down the Mississippi River to the Gulf of Mexico. They would then sail to Florida and spend the winter there on the boat. After Steve convinced Kevin to quit his job at the local paper mill, the two were ready to leave in the fall.

Kevin later told me, "It seemed like the thing to do at the time." He was referring to quitting his job. It probably wasn't the smartest thing to do. But, when there's a dream to follow and a sailboat to travel in, reason sometimes takes second place.

As it turned out, the pair did make their voyage. It likely was the greatest adventure of their lives. Somehow, this dream of Kevin and Steve would be a spark. And the spark would light a fire. And that fire would continue to burn in their hearts and in the hearts of those who were influenced by their dreams. As far as I know, that fire still burns to this day.

CHAPTER 2
NAOMI, AN ADVENTURER

It was a cold January evening. My two children, Caleb, 3, and Sarah, 2, had been tucked in bed and were both asleep. Mary, my wife, was pregnant and due to give birth at any time.

Caleb had been born in L'Anse and his birth was so sudden that we barely had time to drive the two miles from our house to the hospital. We didn't even have time to register at the desk. He was being born as the doctor was entering the delivery room. Sarah would be born a year later. Her birth occurred at a slightly slower pace. She gave us time enough to check in at the hospital. But she was delivered not more than a half hour after we arrived.

Now it was time for the birth of our third child. But this time, we didn't live just two miles from the hospital. The trip was more like 20 miles. As we got ready for bed, Mary felt the baby drop lower. Even though it was getting late at night, Mary thought it would be a good idea to go to the hospital and be checked by a doctor. So we called a friend, Brenda De Grave. She came over to watch the two small children. As Mary and I were getting ready to leave, Brenda handed us a quilt. "After how quickly you had your last children, you better take this quilt just in case," she said. We took the quilt. We got in the car and headed for Escanaba.

We were living in the Wilson, Michigan area at the time. I was driving my first new car. It was a 1980 Chevette 4-door. It was January 1982. As I drove the first five miles or so, I replayed in my mind what I would do if the baby started to come before we made it there. I had been a book salesman for about two years now and our company carried a set of medical books that I had been selling. I had read the section on childbirth several times. As I pondered these thoughts something began to happen.

Mary began to go into labor. Her water broke. This signaled that the child was ready to be born at any time. With new urgency I began to accelerate. I didn't want to take any chances knowing how quickly Mary had delivered the first two children. I knew I didn't want to be alone on an empty highway, at midnight in the middle of nowhere, trying to deliver a baby.

In the meantime, Mary began to moan and groan. She was holding her belly and urging me to hurry. I was hurrying as much as I could. After a few more miles the moaning and groaning became more intense, reaching a climax at this point. I was racing toward Escanaba at top speed. Through her groans Mary said, "We're not going to make it."

I pulled the car over to the side of the road. I got out. It was below zero. As I ran to Mary's side of the car I opened the back door on the passenger's side. I flipped the back seat down. The car was a hatchback. So with the seat down there is a sizeable area to lie down. I went to Mary's door and picked her up. I set her down on the quilt we had grabbed when we left the house.

Was I ready for this? Could I do this? As I looked around, there was not another car in sight. I knew the moment was in God's hands and I would do my part. Mary was lying on her back. I was kneeling on the floor. As Mary began to moan and push, the baby reached the birth canal. There was no turning back, no stopping now. The moment of truth had arrived.

Another groan. Another push. I could now see where the baby's head was bulging Mary's skin. I was placing my hands in such a way as to stretch the skin around the birth canal. I was trying to make the opening larger. Another groan and push and the top of the baby's head appeared. I told Mary to keep pushing. Slowly, the baby's head came clearer into view. I held the head in my hand. I encouraged Mary by telling her of the progress. I told her to keep pushing.

I gently pulled at the right times and a tiny body appeared in my hands. I cleared the baby's mouth and she began to cry. She was still attached to the umbilical cord. If you apply a steady, gentle pressure the placenta also clears the birth canal. This is what I did. Mary and I were happy and relieved to see that things had gone so well. I didn't have a knife or scissors to cut the umbilical cord. I ripped some strips of cloth off my shirt and tied them around the cord. Then I wrapped mother and baby in the quilt, which had been a handmade wedding gift to us. Steve Johnson and his girlfriend Chris (Christine Louise) Burnis had given it to us. Chris was the girlfriend Steve had named his boat after.

And so, Naomi "The Adventurer" was born. Perhaps this dramatic beginning would foreshadow the path of life that lay ahead for Naomi. I got back in behind the wheel and drove the car into Escanaba. We decided it was best to go to the hospital to have Mary and Naomi checked by a doctor. We were happy to have a little baby by Mary's side. As we pulled into the emergency room parking area, I didn't see anyone around. I went inside and again saw no one. So I walked farther. Finally, I found a nurse. I told her that we had just delivered a baby in the car on the way there. She seemed surprised that I was so calm, having just delivered a baby. Getting the necessary help, we got Mary and the baby checked in. They would stay overnight for observation.

It was 3 a.m. I was just starting to feel relieved that everything was under control. Just then, a nurse at the desk told me I had a telephone call. It was Brenda, the babysitter. She told me that soon after we left she was getting ready to go to bed. But then she smelled smoke. She went into the kitchen and saw smoke coming out from around the chimney.

Brenda became concerned when she couldn't get the smoke to stop billowing out from the chimney. She called her husband, Terry. He is a heating and plumbing installer. Walking back to the bedroom, she noticed a tiny light coming from a small hole in the attic door. The light was the bright orange glow of fire. The entire attic was ablaze. Brenda told me that she got the children out safely to the neighbor's house. She called the fire department. Quick work on the part of the firefighters saved the house. But I wouldn't be able to stay at home that night. The children and I would stay at Brenda and Terry's house until repairs to the house could be made.

It was a night of adventure—the night our second daughter was born. It seems adventure truly would be in her blood from that day forward. And the fire of the dream would continue to burn through Naomi "The Adventurer."

CHAPTER 3
EARLY SAILING ADVENTURES

A couple of years after Naomi's birth I decided to move back to Manistique. My high school friends and of course, my parents and brother Butch lived there. Finding a small house in the country to rent, we made the move. It was fall and with winter coming I was able to get some wood cut. We settled into our new place with only a part-time job. I needed to find other work. Cutting wood in the winter helped supplement my meager income. It was backbreaking work, especially for someone not familiar with the trade. An experienced man felling trees could drop them very accurately. I could not. This resulted in much more time and effort being spent. It also resulted in less money because we were paid by the piece or "stick" of wood that was cut and piled. The job was neither easy nor profitable. But it helped keep us going.

A quarter-mile or so down the street from my house lived Paul Johnson. Paul was one of my high school chums and a cousin to Steve Johnson, the sailor. Steve's sailing bug had already bitten Paul. He was a fledgling sailor that first summer. I remember Paul's first sailboat. It was a 12-foot Snipe made of plywood. The boat leaked terribly. Paul had tarred the bottom, but the boat still leaked badly. When he pulled the boat up to the shore he would lift it up onto some concrete blocks. He did this so the boat wouldn't fill up with water when he left it sitting for a few days. But Paul wanted the bottom of the boat to remain wet so the moisture would let the wood expand. Paul described it as "swelling."

After my first winter working in the woods I decided that lumberjacking was definitely not the career choice for me. I decided to do something else. Something I'd done in the past. After I was out of high school I had started a small painting business. I ran the business for a couple of years before trying some other trades. I still had a few ladders and small tools. I strapped them onto my small station wagon. I put an ad in the newspaper and I was back in business.

It was on one of my painting jobs that I found a boat for myself. I was working for an elderly lady named Mrs. Firring. She lived in Curtis in the next county east. I discovered the small sailboat in her barn. The boat was a 9-foot fiberglass "Shell Lake" boat shaped like a pumpkin seed. The boat was in "like new" condition. It had a red top and a white bottom and one sail. I thought the boat was beautiful. I asked Mrs. Firring about it. She said that it had only been used a few times. She said her husband had tipped it over. That was the last time they had used it. The boat had sat in the barn for about ten years.

I struggled during the conversation. But finally, I mustered up enough courage to ask her it she would sell it to me. Mrs. Firring told me she would think about it. She said she'd give me an answer the next day. The following morning I came to work wondering if she would sell the boat. If so, how much would she want for it? Would I be able to afford it? I would soon find out.

I arrived at work and began painting for the day. I waited for Mrs. Firring to come outside. Every moment I painted I wondered what she would say. Finally, she came out and cheerfully bid me, "Good day." We talked about the progress I was making painting and the work yet to be done. I couldn't wait any longer. So I asked her about the boat.

She started out telling me that she still had the original purchase paperwork. She said the boat had cost $900 when they bought it ten years ago from the factory in Shell Lake, Wisconsin. Then she told me she would sell the boat for $125. That doesn't sound like a lot of money to most folks. But to me, a starving painter with a wife and three small children, it was a big investment.

I told Mrs. Firring that I would like to have the boat if she could take the money from what she would owe me for painting. She said she would. I nearly leaped for joy. After work that evening we loaded the boat on top of my station wagon. I tied it down. The boat looked very smart on top of my wagon. A millionaire with a new yacht couldn't have been more proud.

I couldn't wait to show my new boat to Steve and Paul. So the first chance I got I brought the boat to Indian Lake. Steve Johnson lived with his parents on the shore there. They lived near Arrowhead Point, the most beautiful and most protected place on the lake.

It seemed that every summer after I got that first boat Arrowhead Point was like a magnet. The family and I would spend many days learning to sail there. The boat, although small, was quite roomy. In addition to having a sail, the boat was equipped with a new set of oars. Paul and Steve gave me some general instructions. The rest I would learn through observation and experimentation.

I remember times when I would just sail alone, especially in rough weather. I stayed mostly inside of the point to avoid large waves. Indian Lake was a big lake that was about 5 miles across and 7 or 8 miles long. The lake was known to whip up into huge waves rather suddenly. So you had to be careful.

We often had picnics on the point. That way the family could enjoy the day while I would sail. I remember one experience in particular when we all were in the boat. Sarah, Caleb, Naomi, Mary and I were all in the 9-foot boat. The lake was rather calm. We were about a half-mile from shore sailing along very slowly with the combined weight of all of us in the boat. I looked to the shore. I saw something in the water about halfway between us and the shore. I pointed it out to the others, looking closer. We could make out the head of a dog swimming toward us. It was our family pet Sheba, a Norwegian elkhound. She had decided to join us out in the boat.

We were concerned for her safety swimming such a long distance. So we called to her to encourage her. She got nearer to the boat. Finally, she got close enough so that I could reach over to help her in. We were all overjoyed to have her safe in the boat. But in our already overcrowded boat we didn't really need a wet dog. Of course, the first thing she did was start shaking off. We all laughed and screamed as the spray showered us.

That type of family fun was the way many days were spent on Indian Lake. And with those days, my knowledge of sailing increased.

CHAPTER 4
VALHALLA

I've noticed something about sailors. There is a natural desire when one starts sailing to own a bigger boat to sail on bigger seas and to be the captain of your own ship. Paul Johnson was going through this. The fledgling sailor was always keeping his eyes open for what would become his next boat.

I remember the first time I saw the boat. It was a 26-foot plywood craft, overlaid with fiberglass with a small cabin on it. The story surrounding the boat's creation is that it had been built by some city police officers from Gladstone, Michigan. They had reportedly been sailing it out on Lake Michigan when a sudden strong wind knocked the boat on its side, nearly capsizing it. The experience frightened the owners so much that the boat was never used again. The mast and sails were sold. The boat sat on a makeshift trailer in a vacant lot where it was left to decay. Paul spotted the boat and asked about it. He was able to buy it for $125. It seems that $125 was the going price for the boats we could afford within our circle of friends. Paul had hauled it home and backed it into the woods behind his house. That's where I thought it would stay.

When Paul showed the boat to me there was a hole in the bottom the size of a coffee table. That was how we got into the boat, by climbing a small ladder up through the hole into what was supposed to be the cockpit of the boat. Paul showed me the small cabin. It had a bunk, a small desk and a dresser. It was nice to see a boat with a cabin on it because in our league of boat owners this was pretty high-class. But there was no mast, nor sails, on the boat. Considering the amount of work that might be needed to ready the boat, I really never thought I'd see it float, much less sail under its own power. Paul later admitted that he wasn't too sure either.

If it hadn't been for Steve's boat building enthusiasm the boat would still be in his backyard. Steve would often be seen headed to Paul's house with a bunch of materials for the boat-building project. I guess I should never underestimate what a dreamer can do—especially when two dreamers get working together on the same project. By the end of summer, they had the hole patched. The bottom had been coated in fiberglass and a large concrete keel was added for ballast and stability. The boat was finally ready to be launched. Although it had no sails or mast, the boat was all fresh and painted white. Steve used his artistic touch to add some deep blue stripes along the length of the boat. This work culminated in some blue and gold scrollwork on the bow. The boat looked quite nice. It was a far cry from the scrap that I'd seen that spring in Paul's backyard.

The following year, Steve and Paul continued to work on the sailboat. Paul had picked up a used 32-foot mast boom and sails. They fitted the items onto the boat with all the stays and rigging. The finished product was a beautiful 26-foot sloop. Her name was painted attractively on her stern: *The Valhalla*. Steve and Paul—being of Scandinavian descent—named the boat after the Viking heaven of Norse mythology. And heaven is what it would be. That boat brought years of friendship and pleasure to all of us.

It was about this time that Paul got into an accident with his car and alcohol may have been a factor. Paul made up his mind that he'd had enough drinking. That was a good decision. I think that his wife Janet was about ready to send him packing. But from that day forward Paul put his energy, heart and soul into his boat. As it turned out, *The Valhalla* would be excellent therapy for him. It also brought his family together and drew a lot of other people to the sailing world.

The day came for launching *The Valhalla* as a full-fledged sailboat. A group of friends helped Paul step the mast, tighten the rigging and launch the boat. She was the biggest sailboat on Indian Lake. I'm sure Paul and Steve were the proudest boat owners around. They would keep the boat at Arrowhead Point.

Steve's cousin Kevin Thorrell was caretaker of the Old Arrowhead Inn. He had made arrangements for Paul and Steve to keep *The Valhalla* in a slip at the Old Arrowhead Inn dock. That is probably the best spot to keep a boat on the whole lake. I was quite common to find Steve or Paul out sailing or tied up at the dock. Often, Paul would sleep on the boat at night. Arrowhead became the place to be. A certain group of friends would be drawn there, year after year for about ten years, while the boat was kept there. There were cookouts, picnics and sailboat races. And yes, Paul was quite the organizer. At one point during those years there was a race held every other Sunday afternoon.

The races were the kind that involved whatever floated and had sails on it. The wide-ranging boat collection was started racing with a flag and the sound of a gun. The gun was usually Paul's shotgun. I think that those were some of the best days of our lives. They were not only good days for us, but for our families and friends also. Ten years for a boat that I thought would never float. I told Paul once that the boat changed his life and the lives of his family members for the better. I would like to say it now for everyone who reads this book that it also helped change my life and my children's lives for the better too. Thank you Steve and Paul and Kevin. I hope that someday we may all sail together in Valhalla for eternity.

CHAPTER 5
EARLY MEMORIES OF LAKE SUPERIOR

As far back in my mind as I can remember, there is Lake Superior with its cool breeze, the crashing of the waves along the shore and the sound of gulls calling in the distance.

I remember there were two white buildings. One was called "The Bungalow." It was a beautiful mansion with seven white pillars across the front. The Bungalow was owned by famous auto giant Henry Ford. The house overlooked Lake Superior. The second building was located close by. This building was the caretaker's cottage and my grandparents' home. My grandparents were Albert and Ingaborg Westman.

There was a white fence around the neatly kept grounds where my grandfather worked as a caretaker. There also was a beautiful flower garden that he kept well. In the center of the garden there was a pedestal made from round Lake Superior stones joined together with mortar. On top of the pedestal sat a faded brass sundial, which was always a point of interest for my brothers, my sisters and me.

I clearly remember driving to and from Grandma's house because it was so interesting. To get there we had to drive through a ghost town called Pequaming. I would sit up on the edge of the car seat and look around with wonder as we drove past boarded-up old buildings, long overgrown and neglected.

As we passed the water tower and the old schoolhouse, my mother would point out each building. She would tell us who had lived there before and what had been located in each building. The Ford Motor Company had owned the town site. The company had a large mill located there for producing wooden parts for automobiles. When Ford stopped using wooden parts, the mill was closed down in 1942. This left Pequaming a ghost town.

I was six years old when my grandfather retired. He moved from the caretaker's cottage to a small house along the bay. The house was located between Pequaming and L'Anse. It was there that we really got a feel for what it was like to live on the big lake. My grandfather had just built a small house for his retirement years. He had built a log cabin earlier in life before he married Grandma. The new house was right next to the cabin.

So when we went to visit, all eight of us kids would stay in the cabin. The cabin was heated with a wood stove. In the kitchen, there was a wood cook stove. Many cool Lake Superior mornings were spent getting dressed near the wood stove.

Before breakfast, my brother Butch and I would get up and go down to the lakeshore. It was always interesting to see the many faces of the lake, with its cold, clear waters, so wild and untamed. On calm days, we could skip rocks on the water and walk along the rocky shore. On stormy days, we would watch the awesome power of the huge waves crashing into the beach.

Grandpa had a large garden up on the hill overlooking the lake. He and Grandma grew just about all of their own produce. Grandpa had also built a large root cellar to keep vegetables and jars of home-canned goods like wild blueberries that we would use for our pancakes in the morning. Grandma and Grandpa sure knew something about living.

Next door to my grandparents was "the farm" which was owned by my Uncle Oscar Westman and my Aunt Helvi. The farm had been the homestead of my great-grandparents. Uncle Oscar and Aunt Helvi still had a cow that they would milk by hand. They also had chickens and a pig. It wasn't until years later that they acquired electricity. There was an icehouse down by the lake. There was a certain feeling of serenity and a kind of self-reliance I felt there along the lakeshore.

Across the driveway stood the "old house," a hand-hewn log house that had belonged to my great-grandparents. They say it's the oldest house in Baraga County. The house still stands there today. It was a wonderful place for us kids. The house was like our own private museum with all the interesting things it contained. I remember seeing a loom for weaving rugs, an old trunk filled with tanned animal hides, an electric belt for curing arthritis and a wooden long bow that my cousin Terry would challenge us with to see if we were strong enough to string it. There was also an old brass bed upstairs. Sometimes my older brother Mike and my cousin Terry would sleep there. In the morning, some of us younger kids would go sneak up the stairs to visit, only to be frightened to near death by one of them leaping out at us unexpectedly, covered with the old bear skin rug.

When we wanted fish from the lake, my Uncle Oscar would "set the net." He would row out with the boat and place a fish net into the water. Then, in the morning, he would pull it up to see what kind of fish had been caught.

I remember on one occasion, my uncle Oscar had won a large wooden rowboat in town. When he brought it to the farm, he and my grandfather fashioned a mast sail and rudder for the boat. I remember its white painted hull and wooden gunnels. I think my uncle had named the boat *Diane* after his daughter.

On another of my most memorable days on Lake Superior, my mother and dad took all of us kids (there was eight of us) to visit my Aunt Ann and Dr. Guy. They lived in a lighthouse. Yes, a real lighthouse. It was the Sand Point Lighthouse on Keweenaw Bay. The brick lighthouse was built in 1878. It made a beautiful home and an interesting place to visit. We all spent the day on the beach. The kids all played in the water so long they started to turn blue. After supper, Dr. Guy took us up the stairs to the lantern room of the lighthouse. Perhaps this is where my interest in Great Lakes maritime history began. As he opened the door to the catwalk outside I was filled with awe and wonder. We were actually in the top of a real lighthouse.

I also remember that my father sometimes brought his 18-foot powerboat when we went to visit at Grandpa and Grandma's house. There were days Dad would use the boat to pull on water skis anyone who felt courageous enough to brave the cold water. He would also take us fishing. On one of the best trips, we fished near Huron Bay. It was so awesome. The Huron Mountains were in the background. And of course, there were the Huron Islands. There is just something about islands that is so fascinating. They invite your curiosity to explore.

So off we went toward the islands. They were barely visible at first. Then they seemed to grow out of the horizon as we drew nearer. This same fascination inspired by the islands would lure me again years later when I sailed to these same Huron Islands with my daughter Naomi. There was a beautiful lighthouse on a towering rocky peak of the island. My father docked the boat in a small harbor and we made our way up a gravel path to the lighthouse. The U.S. Coast Guard still manned the lighthouse back then in the 1960s. A lonely guardsman welcomed us by giving us a personal tour of the light station and its operations. It was the highlight of our day.

It was times like these that make life worth living. Thank you Dad, for bringing us there. Thank you Grandma and Grandpa, for choosing to live there. Thank you God, for making Lake Superior a part of my life and my heritage. These are some of my early memories of the lake. They are memories that would call me back; back to the magical and beautiful lake called Superior. Perhaps it was at this early age in my childhood that my love for boats began. Maybe my Norwegian and Swedish ancestry on my mother's side awakened some distant Viking heritage and love of the sea.

My memories of Lake Superior are like living pearls on a great necklace. I have shared a few of these pearls. But before I go on, there is one story that I must share. Years had passed and Grandma and Grandpa were now gone. My cousin Terry owned their house by the lake. It was now the early 1970s. I was growing from an adolescent into a man. As was true of many young people during that time period, there seemed to be a lack of direction in my life and in the lives of my friends.

I made a few visits to Grand Marais, a beautiful place about 45 miles east of Munising on Superior's shore. There are great sand dunes there that stretch for miles. The dunes are dotted with small patches of forest. As you look out over the lake from these lofty mounds, the water and the sun and sky seem to open before you. Your soul seems to drift toward the horizon. You can almost sense eternity.

I think I was 17 at the time. I'm not sure where, but I read some place that it was here on these Grand Sable Dunes that Native American Indians would come to fast and pray to the Great Spirit. I had also heard that Jesus and some of his prophets had fasted and prayed when they were seeking direction in their lives. Somehow, I came to the conclusion that I would have a buddy of mine drop me off at the dunes. There I would fast and pray to the Great Spirit. For four long and lonely days I camped there on the dunes alone with nature. Alone with nothing more than a tent and a sleeping bag, days can seem very long when you don't have meal times to break things up. There's also no one to talk to. No one, that is, except yourself and God.

It was springtime and the new leaves swayed in the cool spring breezes. On the fourth day I was feeling weak from hunger. I had no water to drink so I became very thirsty. I decided to go down to the lake to get some water. The problem was there was a 350-foot drop to the lake. In my weakened condition I struggled to climb down to the water's edge. The water in the lake was cool and refreshing. But the hike back to the top was exhausting. When I got back to my camp I was so tired. I lay down outside my tent on my belly. I had my head propped up on my arms. I was facing a small campfire, too tired to move.

I lay there awhile and was just beginning to dose. All of a sudden, I heard a noise that startled me. I looked up just in time to see a deer jumping over my head and my campfire. I turned to watch as the deer landed and turned to face me. The animal was now about 10 yards from my campsite. He stood there making gestures toward me with his front hooves, almost playfully. I spoke in a gentle voice. I asked him why he had come. He stayed close by for some time. The whole while I was watched with wonder. I could hardly believe my eyes.

Finally, after awhile, the deer disappeared into the forest leaving me to wonder. I don't think that anyone else could say that they have ever seen anything like it. Some years later, I spoke to a Native American medicine man. He suggested that the experience was more than just a natural occurrence. He said that the deer was not acting like a normal deer. He said that this was actually a "spirit deer." This deer was a sign to me that the Great Spirit would guide me in life's journey. The medicine man told me my character was like that of the deer. Gently, I would lead my family and friends on their life's journey. My understanding of this experience is that I would be blessed. And my life truly has been blessed. So it was in both my childhood and as I became an adult, the big lake spoke to me. It left an impression on my soul that would never be erased.

CHAPTER 6
SAILING ON LAKE SUPERIOR

You don't just put your 16-foot sailboat into Lake Superior one day and say, "I think I'll sail around Lake Superior today."

A couple of years after my divorce I bought a house near Munising— a small town on the shores of Munising Bay—that I would launch my sailboat in Lake Superior. At the time, I actually had two catamaran sailboats. One was a 16-foot Hobie Cat. The second boat was a 15-foot Sol Cat. I kept the Hobie Cat down on Indian Lake where I still sailed with Steve and the Indian Lake Yacht Club. I kept the Sol Cat on Lake Superior.

Many days were spent sailing on Munising Bay. The water of Lake Superior, although it's cold, has an almost irresistible attraction. The water is clear and seemingly alive with an invigorating energy all its own. It wasn't long before I was spending most of my time sailing on the lake. It just so happened that my girlfriend's brother Jimmers was into racing Hobie Cats. That winter he invited me to go with him to Mexico and work as a crew for him in the Hobie Cat midwinter's west races. Actually, he had invited his sister Cindy. But she declined. So as a noble gesture, I volunteered.

Off to Mexico we went. When we arrived, we set up camp at a campground on the beach at San Felipe on the *Sea of Cortez*. There were hundreds of boats. Altogether, I think there were 215. Their brightly colored sails were lined up along the beach. It was quite a spectacle. We set up our boat and we were ready to race.

The next morning, the races began. Jimmer was a pretty good sailor and I learned a lot of new tricks from him. We placed 8th, 4th and 1st .We probably would have gotten a trophy, but the last race was cancelled due to problems with the race committee's boat. Although I enjoyed the races, I really rather would have spent more time exploring the coastline of the Baja Peninsula. The serenity was awesome. There were huge mountains and beautiful desert meeting the shoreline. They invited me to explore. But alas, we only sailed circles in a bay congested with boats and people. I was a country boy and it was in my heart to explore. So I did rent a small 3-wheeled all-terrain vehicle and did some exploring. But I really thought it would be nicer to explore by sea.

The next summer, Jimmers was planning on coming up to Munising with his boat. He said he found a good deal on a Hobie 16 that was in good shape. So I sold both my Hobie 16 and my Sol Cat 15-footer and bought the newer Hobie. Jimmers made a set of "wings" which were like two benches on each side of the boat. They were made from aluminum tubing with canvas stretched over the top for seats. These wings greatly increased the usefulness and comfort of the catamaran. That summer, we spent about two weeks sailing together. But, the highlight of the summer was a sailboat trip along the Pictured Rocks National Lakeshore to Grand Marais.

It was a beautiful summer day. We sailed out of Munising at about 9 a.m. We had two Hobie Cats. Jimmers and my son Caleb were on one boat. Cindy and I were on the other. We left the shelter of the harbor, and ventured out into the open waters of Lake Superior. This was a dream come true to be traveling on Lake Superior's "Shipwreck Coast." We were riding along some of the most awesome scenery in the world. We were on 16-foot boats powered only by wind. All I can say is the experience was indescribable. Our boats seemed dwarfed by the giant rocky cliffs.

We passed Grand Island—that great island of beauty and adventure. We moved along the massive rock cliffs of Pictured Rocks. The winds were light as we sailed past Miners Castle and Miners Beach. But as we rounded Portal Rock, the breeze freshened. We took off like a rocket. The only difficulty we had was as we passed Au Sable Point Lighthouse. Terrific offshore winds coming off the Grand Sable Dunes rocked our boats. The winds almost caused us to capsize. But we sailed on.

One thing I learned about sailing with Jimmers is that you're always in a race. So when Cindy and I reached Grand Marais about 15 minutes ahead of Jimmers and Caleb, I think he gained respect for me as a sailor. We were having dinner at the restaurant by 1 p.m. We covered the 40 or so miles in only four hours. Not bad. Traveling at 10 mph for a sailboat was quite impressive. We finished lunch and headed out to our boats only to find a thunderstorm moving in. Securing the sailboats, we crawled under them for protection from the rain and wind. Then we all took about an hour-long nap while we waited out the storm.

The weather quickly improved and we were soon on our way back to Munising. As we started out the weather only gave us light winds. So travel was slow at times. But, about the time we reached Miners Castle, a sudden gale blew in from the northwest. In an instant we were in huge waves.

Jimmers and Caleb were ahead of us this time. They were also farther out at sea. Rather than getting beat up in the huge waves, Cindy and I opted to land the boat at Miners Beach.

One advantage of the catamaran is that with the wind pushing on the sails we were shoved right through the treacherous breakers onto the beach. Landing in a conventional boat would have been very dangerous. The Hobie Cat's shallow draft made the twin hulls seem like a pair of sled runners that helped make landing possible in heavy seas. We pulled the boat far up on land, grabbed the sails and our life jackets and bummed a ride home with some tourists. Our hair was wild and our faces wind-whipped. But we were beaming with smiles as we recounted the tale of our journey to our hosts.

When we returned to Munising, we waited on the dock at Cindy's parents' place. We had lost sight of Jimmers and Caleb. We were concerned that they may be in danger. It was getting dark and we could see no sign of them. Finally, we heard them answer our shouts. We were soon all reunited on the shoreline, happy that all of us had survived the storm.

It was the success of that day's journey that was the beginning of an idea. I began to think that if a person were to pack right, why couldn't they make a journey around all of Lake Superior? What a trip that would be! I would love to pilot a 16-foot sailboat around the lake that has claimed hundreds of ships, including the mighty Edmund Fitzgerald. To be able to pull the boat up out of the water and camp on the most beautiful and rugged shoreline in the world would be great. Imagine. What a trip that would be!

CHAPTER 7

CRAZY

It was about this time that my painting company was contracted to restore the Seul Choix Point Lighthouse, a beautiful lighthouse and keeper's quarters on the shore of Lake Michigan, near the town of Gulliver, Michigan. This job ultimately would change my life.

The best part of summer was spent at Seul Choix Point (pronounced Sis-shwaw). After learning a few basic chords and songs on the guitar, I began composing some of my own songs. The surroundings and rich history of the lighthouse began to inspire me to write my first, and one of my best-known Great Lakes ballads entitled, *The Ballad of Seul Choix Point Lighthouse*. While working on the lighthouse for nearly six weeks, I stayed in my camper trailer on the point. Rising early, I would sit and watch the sun rise over the lake and would play my guitar. Soon, some of the word pictures began to form in my mind: *Where the forest meets the water cool, where the fisherman and the Indian sang their songs in the night, by the firelight—Seul Choix.* It would be a few weeks before more lyrics would come.

Many fine evenings were spent at the old Deerfield Resort and Restaurant. It was there that the owners, Glen and Marilyn Fisher, told stories of the history of the lighthouse. Marilyn was also the head of the Gulliver Historical Society, which had hired me to work on the lighthouse. She was a treasure trove of information about the history of the area. When I told her and Glen that I was thinking of writing a song about the lighthouse, they encouraged the idea, suggesting lyrics. Even Jodi, the waitress, suggested a line. My daughter, Sarah, also added some lyrics. They all helped tell the story. Finally, as the work on the light was completed, the song was also finished.

The Ballad of Seul Choix Point Lighthouse

Spoken: The story is told of some French sailors who were caught in a storm out on Lake Michigan. Back in the days when the French controlled much of the fur trade on the Upper Great Lakes. During the storm, the sailors realized there was little hope for survival. But just when their

*hope was just about given out, they saw a point of land and they knew if
they could get around it, the would be saved. So it was their only choice
to get around that point. And the French words for "only choice" are seul
choix. And so the name Seul Choix Point has been that name to this day.*

*Where the forest meets the water's cool
Where the fisherman and the Indian sang their songs
In the night, by the firelight—Seul Choix
Where the French of old, so the story's told,
Sought a solace there from the storm at Seul Choix
It was their only choice—Seul Choix*

*As the days passed by, they built a tower high
Flashing out into the evening sky at Seul Choix
They built a tower high—Seul Choix
And they laughed and danced into the night
While the fiddler played his songs with delight at Seul Choix
They danced into the night at Seul Choix*

*And if you listen to the evening wind
You can hear their voices singing again at Seul Choix
Hear their voices sing—Seul Choix
Where the eagle flies,' cross the open skies
Great Spirit touch my eyes that I might see
Your beauty there where the eagle flies—Seul Choix
Au dieu bien venue is what the sailors say
Au dieu bien venue—Seul Choix
Au dieu bien venue is what the sailors say
Au dieu bien venue—Seul Choix*

The historical society would later make a video about the history of
Seul Choix Point. Don Hermanson of Keweenaw Video Productions
asked if he could use the song in the video. But he said he needed a professional recording and suggested a studio that would do a good job.
Before I knew it, I had my first CD recorded. The success of the CD and
the experience of working on the lighthouse spurred my interest in mar-

itime history. Over time, I became not only a Great Lakes sailor, but also a Great Lakes balladeer. The following year, I produced my second CD called *Legends of the Great Lakes.*

Jesus once told a parable about a grain of mustard seed. He said that even though the seed was small, it would one day grow up to be a great plant. So it was with my desire to sail around Lake Superior—the largest freshwater lake in the world. The idea was small. But over time it began to grow and eventually it came true. But the process didn't happen overnight.

I got a friend of mine named Tom Nolta interested in sailing. After he sailed with me a couple of times, he bought a used 16-foot Prindle catamaran for $650. I helped him get the boat set up and properly rigged. Occasionally he allowed me to take it out sailing when he wasn't using it. As I became more familiar with the boat, I began to prefer some of its features over those of my Hobie Cat. One feature that I liked was that the Prindle had larger hulls. It was less likely to "pitch pole." That is, the front hull could get forced under the water when the boat was moving ahead at a high rate of speed. This would cause the boat to flip head over heels or "pitch pole." I had done this once in a race on Indian Lake on the Fourth of July.

Just after the start of the race, I was passing all of the other boats like they were standing still, passing the leading crew. I watched their boat as we flew past at an incredible speed. All of a sudden the front of my boat was underwater and we were tossed into the lake. That was something I didn't really want to have happen on a trip around Lake Superior. I also thought the Prindle would be able to carry a little more weight than the Hobie.

The following spring I asked Tom if he would be interest in selling the Prindle. He really hadn't used the boat. So he said he'd sell it to me for $650. I took the boat home. I gave it a paint job and some new parts. But most importantly, I bought a brand new set of "wings" for the boat. If you remember, "wings" are a framework or aluminum tube and canvas benches off to each side of the boat. The wings greatly increased the amount of room and comfort on the boat. Another addition I made was a motor mount and a small gas motor—a 1½-horsepower Tanaka. I think it only weighed 11 pounds.

The day came to launch the boat. It was early summer and Naomi and I launched the boat at Sand Point on Munising Bay. It would have been nice if I had taken the time to register the boat and put numbers on it. But when it's a beautiful summer day and the state permit offices are closed, I figured: "Why sweat the small stuff." It wasn't until 3 p.m. when we finally set sail. With a steady 15-mph. breeze, Naomi and I shoved off. We got under full sail. The breeze was great. It took us out the East Channel along the Pictured Rocks to Miners Castle. What a perfect day for sailing. We were elated. The boat looked like new with our new motor and new wings. And with this good wind we felt like we could sail around the big lake that day. But instead, we would settle for sailing around Grand Island.

So from Miners Castle we turned the boat toward Grand Island. Although I had sailed around the island in the past, it was still no small feat. It's about 40 miles around the island. I believe it is one of the most beautiful places in the world. The deep clear water reveals a rugged and awesome underwater world that is the home of the Alger Underwater Preserve. The preserve contains several interesting shipwrecks including the *Bermuda,* the *Manhattan,* the *George,* the *Smith-Moor,* the *Kiowa* and many others.

As we passed Trout Bay and approached the cliff of the North Point Lighthouse, we saw a powerboat approaching. It drew closer and I saw that it was the game warden.

"Oh, oh," I said.

I knew he was going to stop and check us. But we were both in such high spirits that I figured even a ticket couldn't spoil our day. The game warden pulled alongside us and asked for our registration. I explained that I had just launched the boat for the first time and that I hadn't registered it yet. He then asked if I had a radio, flare gun and a throwable floatation device. I answered that I didn't know I was required to carry all that stuff. Then he questioned our sanity about sailing around Grand Island on a 16-foot sailboat. I assured him that although it was our first time sailing our new boat it was not our first trip out. He shook his head in disbelief.

As he drove off he said, "Get that thing registered ASAP!"

"Yes, sir."

Off he went. I wonder what he would have thought if he knew we were thinking about sailing around the entire lake on this boat? I asked Naomi what she thought he was thinking.

"I'm sure he would have thought we were crazy. Heck, he already does," she said.

On we sailed around Grand Island and into Munising Bay. The big orange sun was drifting low in the sky, marking the end of a perfect day of sailing. We had covered about 50 miles since 3 p.m. that afternoon.

"Not bad for an afternoon sail," I said.

In my mind, this trip had confirmed my belief that it was possible for Naomi and I to sail around Superior.

CHAPTER 8

TRIAL RUN

The following summer I launched the boat. Over the course of time I had refined my packing method to strapping waterproof dry bags to the topside of the wings. This solved the problem of keeping things dry and having enough space to put things in. As you might imagine, there isn't a heck of a lot of storage space on this kind of boat. I had also outfitted the boat with a 3-horsepower Tanaka motor, rather than the 1½-horsepower model, for better performance.

The summer was quickly passing. If I was going to go around the lake I needed to get going. The problem I had was that I worked every week-day during the summer with my painting and decorating business. Time was at a premium. I decided I would try making the trip in sections. The first section would be from Munising to Batchawana Bay in Ontario, Canada. This place is near where my brother Butch has a camp that he goes to almost every weekend. The plan for the first leg was simple. I would sail the boat up to Canada. Once there, I would park it and catch a ride back home with my brother. Then, in a week or two, I would have my brother drop me off at the boat. I could then continue on my journey. That way I wouldn't have to take so much time off from work all at once.

The day finally came for the first leg of the journey. It arrived with no fanfare. My son Caleb and I sailed out of Munising Bay toward Grand Marais. The weather was fine. The wind was great, carrying us on our way. We stopped at Au Sable Point Lighthouse to do some sightseeing before heading off again to Grand Marais. It was a place we knew well as we had been hired to do several restoration projects there on the light-house property.

So we had learned first-hand some of the interesting history of the lighthouse. One of those stories is the wreck of the *Kiowa*. The year was 1929. A November storm caught Capt. Alex T. Young out on the open lake. His 251-foot, 1300-horsepower ship was no match for Superior in a nasty mood.

The ship's cargo of flax shifted, causing the ship to list and take on water. The captain panicked. Thinking all was lost, he ordered 10 men into the lifeboat, at gunpoint, according to some reports. He left the rest of the crew of 23 to their own fates with the ship.

But the lifeboat immediately capsized as it was being launched, spilling the captain and crew into icy waves. One man climbed back into the lifeboat as the captain and four others drowned. Six men were pulled back onto the ship.

Drifting helplessly, the ship struck ground about five miles west of the lighthouse, but out of the keeper's view. A group of hunters from Grand Marais—Richard Chilson and his son Charles and Earl Howay—spotted the ship, while they waited out the storm near Twelvemile Beach.

As the storm moderated, they launched their small powerboat through the rolling seas and took some of the *Kiowa*'s crew to the safety of the lighthouse. The lightkeepers then used the fog signal to alert the Coast Guard station in Grand Marais.

When the Coast Guard failed to respond, the two hunters then returned to the ship, towing a boat from the lighthouse to take off the rest of the crew. As they returned to the lighthouse, the Coast Guard finally arrived, taking the crewmen aboard from the hunters' boat. They also picked up the remaining crewmen from the *Kiowa*.

One sore spot to our local heroes is that in the official telegram to the Coast Guard District office, no mention was made of the hunters' part in the rescue. As for the crewman who was able to climb back into the lifeboat, he was found by a fish tug, drifting in the open lake. He had frozen to death.

The anchor and two of the bronze propeller blades from the *Kiowa* are now part of a beautiful memorial fountain in front of the Peoples State Bank in Munising.

Barbara Hubbard of Grand Marais, daughter of Richard Chilson, shared her account of this story with me. She promises an in-depth account in a book she hopes to publish soon.

It seems that every time I sail from Au Sable Point to Grand Marais I experience strong gusting winds coming off the great Au Sable Dunes. This trip was no exception. The strong wind brought rougher conditions. But we were making good time as we approached the Grand Marais Harbor entrance.

The wind and waves grew even stronger. We had sailed past Grand Marais about five miles when all of a sudden, something snapped. Instantly, my jib sail fell down into the water. Immediately, I headed for shore. So there I was—only one day out and I was already cold and wet.

My boat had a damaged sail and we were limping to shore through big waves. I must admit that at this point I was wondering if I hadn't bit off more than I could chew.

When we reached the shore Caleb and I pulled the boat up. I was very discouraged. But Caleb was very upbeat about things. That helped me be more positive. We repaired the sail, had something to eat and we were on our way again. We sailed until dark then took a break on the shore. We debated whether to make camp there or continue on. As soon as it started getting dark the winds died down to almost nothing. We decided to take the sails down and try motoring. I hadn't used the motor much. So this was a good chance to try it out and put it to the test.

We motored off into the night. We kept going until we saw a navigation light shining. We thought it was Whitefish Point in the distance. We figured we would pull up and camp. Then, in the morning, we'd travel the short distance to Whitefish Point before crossing over the international border into Canada.

The next morning we awoke to a beautiful sunrise. There is no place on earth like the Lake Superior shoreline. It is wild and free and very remote. The scenery makes any hardships you might endure well worth the effort. As we got up and started moving around the campsite I noticed some animal tracks leading to the boat. I followed the patterns in the sand. As it turned out, a skunk had gotten into a small bag of food we had left out. That little stinker!

Caleb and I loaded our gear and set sail. There was a fine breeze. But as we started traveling it didn't take long to realize the light we saw the night before was not the Whitefish Point Lighthouse. It was the entrance light at Little Lake Harbor, located several miles to the west of Whitefish Point. So we continued on. We made one stop along the way. That was at the old Vermilion Lifesaving Station.

Because of the large number of shipwrecks along the "Shipwreck Coast" (from Whitefish Point to Grand Island), the government set up four lifesaving stations. The U.S. Lifesaving Service was mainly a rescue operation that saved hundreds of lives of shipwrecked and endangered mariners. We checked out the old buildings at Vermilion with much interest.

The history of the Lifesaving Service, although almost totally unknown and unheard of, is one of America's best-kept secrets. Here is one story that I must share from Captain Trudell, formerly a lifesaving captain. The story was written by Kendrick Kimball and originally appeared in the *Detroit News* on March 17, 1935. Mary Capagrossa of the *Great Lakes Mariner* provided me with this article.

STRANGE DREAM FORETOLD SHIPWRECK

When the wind shrills from the northwest on a dark, moonless night and clouds of spray dance wraith-like over the Grand Marais breakwater, Captain Benjamin Trudell sometimes can be induced to tell the story of "The Man on the Beach."

Mariners far and wide shake their heads over the story's supernatural element. They do not try to explain it. Nor does the captain. Whatever the cause, coincidence or some sort of telepathic communication over 20 miles of roaring water, one of Superior's most tragic disasters was foretold by a dream.

The dream came to Capt. Trudell on an August night in 1892 when a whooping northwest gale wrote oblivion across the logbook of the Western Reserve, "queen of the inland seas," which went down with a loss of 27 lives, including that of Peter G. Minch, Cleveland millionaire-owner, his wife and two small children.

Capt. Trudell, commander of the Grand Marais lifesaving station for 20 years, and now retired, was then a young member of the "navy of hope" at the Deer Park station, on the desolate and uninhabited shore between Grand Marais and Whitefish Point. Beyond lay one of the "graveyards of the lakes."

Launching their surfboats from wheels, the lifesavers rowed through ranges of foam-crested mountains to the wrecks grinding to pieces on the shoals. It was brawn pitted against the elements. They fought their way ahead a foot at a time, deluged with icy water, lashed with spray, nine weary men in a cockteshell, who knew that somewhere in the murkiness, men, women and children awaited their coming.

A Storm in Background

Still bronzed, still rugged and possessing the same voice which boomed orders above the howl of many a storm, Capt. Trudell retoled the story from an armchair in his inn at Grand Marais. The setting was perfect, for old Superior was in an ugly mood. Thick and tattered clouds raced low across the sky, and a "norther" moaned under the eaves.

"It was during my second year in the lifesaving service," said the Captain, born in Bay City and now 63. "Our station was one of four along that lonely stretch of shore. The gale, from the northwest, was one of the worst I experienced. The station creaked and groaned from the buffeting it received, sand swished against the windows and pines tossed so furiously it seemed their roots must give way.

Affected by Dream

"At midnight when I was awakened to go on patrol I leaped from my cot, trembling and perspiring, and glanced about widely, for I had been dreaming of a wreck, a dream so realistic I still fancied myself on the beach. The delusion persisted in spite of my comrades, dressed in oilskins and carrying lanterns, and the familiar surroundings of the dormitory.

"What's the matter, Ben," asked one of the crew.

"I've had a most peculiar dream," I replied. "A ship's going down out there tonight and a lot of people will go with her."

"You're crazy," someone volunteered. "A sensible skipper would stay behind Point Iroquois if he doubted his boat. He wouldn't round Whitefish until the blow was over."

"I shook my head. Mark my words, tomorrow we'll hear of a wreck— a bad one."

"I had dreamed I was walking down the beach through the storm," the captain continued. "I had not gone far before I became aware of another presence—that of a well-dressed man, obviously someone of position. His clothing was of the finest material, his collar of linen, his tie of silk, his moustache neatly trimmed. He stepped out of the spray as if to bar my path, muttering something I could not catch.

"Agitated, he pointed three times over the water with a pleading look. He stood there for perhaps a second, his white and drawn face pressed close to mine, and then melted back into the spray, continuing what was obviously a supplication of help.

"Most of the boys laughed when I described the dream. We patrolled the beach, but found nothing. At breakfast the joking continued and by noon even the commander of the station, Capt. Frahm, joined the fun at my expense.

"This day isn't over yet," I protested. "Maybe you'll change your minds before nightfall."

The Sole Survivor

Hardly had the words left my lips when the lookout reported the approach of a man in the last stages of exhaustion. He was a sailor, wet and bedraggled, who dragged himself through the door by sheer will power, blurted out that he was the only survivor of a floundered vessel, and collapsed.

"The man was Harry Stewart, of Algonac, wheelman on the Western Reserve. Revived by hot drinks, he told how the steamer snapped like a pipe stem in the storm, how he and 18 others took off in a yawl, how the small craft overturned in the surf, and, how he managed to fight his way to shore.

(Peter G. Minch, owner of the Western Reserve) made the boat the flagship of his fleet of 14 vessels that bore the Minch pennon into every port from Kingston to Dulith, and selected her as the safest vehicle for a pleasure cruise for himself and his family.

The vacation party consisted of Minch and his wife, Charles, 10 years old; Florence, 6; his sister-in-law, Mrs. Mary Englebry of Vermillion, Ohio, and the latter's daughter, Bertha. Capt. Albert Myers, of Vermillion, master of the Western Reserve, was a close friend of the Minch and Englebry families, as was his son, Carl, who also made the cruise.

Bound for Two Harbors, Minnesota, for a cargo of ore, the steamer puffed majestically up the Detroit River. Champagne corks popped a salute to calm weather in Lake Huron. With Holiday spirit, Minch and the party smiled and waved at the crowds lining the lock at Sault Ste. Marie to watch the steamer pass through the gateway to Superior.

But the blue waters of Superior were gray and wind-whipped. When Capt, Myers suggested that the Western Reserve take shelter behind Point Iroquois, the owner, with an impatient tug at his mustache, ordered him to push on. Past Whitefish Point went the vessel, disregarding the banked masses of clouds and government signals that promised more severe weather. With a sonorous farewell from her whistle, the doomed ship nosed into the frothing combers that soon were to hammer her to bits.

"About dark she began to labor heavily," Stewart related to his audience of lifesavers. "The crew became uneasy. But Minch was supremely confident."

The Crash

He reassured the huddle of women and children in the salon, terrified by sliding furniture and falling kitchen utensils. He slapped the worried Captain on the back, and joked with the solemn knots of men in the engine room. But the laboring became more apparent and the hull seemed to shiver beneath the assault of the seas.

A terrific crash! The ship quivered from stem to stern! Sharp noises like pistol shots broke above the din of the storm. Lights went out to the popping of rivets, the vessel veered drunkenly, and the decks, black with tumbling water, buckled as if to the explosion of a string of giant firecrackers. Then as if to complete the disintegrations, the mainmast tottered and fell.

"I jumped across a crack in the deck two feet wide to reach the yawl, which contained the Minch party and a portion of the crew," resumed Stewart, now a ship Captain and residing in Algonac.

"The remainder scrambled into a metallic lifeboat partially stove in by the mast. The ship went down in about 10 minutes after we left it."

Lifeboats Capsize

"The lifeboat capsized almost immediately, but we in the yawl managed to save two passengers, the captain's son and the steward. The 19 persons in the yawl proved too heavy a load and we bailed continually with our hats and only pail to keep afloat."

The yawl wallowed bravely through the blackness. Waves clutched within a few inches of the laboring men, the women, silent in their resignation, and the whimpering children. A cry of hope went up when someone spied the light of a steamer to the west. The party shouted and screamed, but their voices were carried away by the gale. They tried to burn a shawl, but it was too wet.

With her lights twinkling a mockery of warmth and security, the steamer passed on, leaving the yawl and its human cargo to the mercy of the breakers ahead."

Thrown Into Surf

"When we struck the surf the yawl capsized in a instant," Stewart

went on. "Mrs. Minch clinging to one of the children, made a desperate effort to swim. I heard Minch cry out as his son was sucked beneath the seas. I put on a life belt I snatched from the bottom of the yawl and struck out for shore with young Myers at my side. He didn't go far, but luck carried me through."

The remainder of the story belongs to Capt. Trudell, who was sent down the beach with a group of searchers. They found the yawl thrown high and dry on the sand, but containing no trace of its former occupants.

Further along the beach was a body. Capt. Trudell, first to reach it, stepped back in amazement, removing his hat mechanically.

"It was the body of a man—the very man, even to the color of his necktie and the pattern of his suit—who appeared to me in the dream," he said. "The body was that of Peter G. Minch, owner of the Western Reserve."

After viewing the lifesaving station, it was on to Whitefish Point. Arriving there, we pulled up the boat. This greatly amused a crowd of people on the shore. Whitefish Point Lighthouse and the Great Lakes Shipwreck Museum draw tourists from all around the country and even the world. They come here to witness the history and beauty of the "Shipwreck Coast." The idea of a couple of sailors on a 16-foot open boat attempting to sail around the great Lake Superior was totally awe-inspiring to the people we talked to.

Meanwhile, the weather was quickly deteriorating as thunderheads loomed up in the distance. We gave my brother a call over on the Canadian side of the lake where he was visiting his wife's parents at their cabin on Goulais Bay. I told him we weren't going to cross that day. We were going to beach the boat and catch a ride into Newberry where he could meet us. He could pick up our gear and give us a ride back home. Back to our jobs, back to our daily routines.

The following weekend I went up to Whitefish Point alone with my sails and my gear. I intended to sail across to Batchawana Bay near my brother Butch's camp. I could meet him there. But on my way to Whitefish Point the rain started coming down steady and it never stopped. So I didn't cross that day either. The next weekend, my buddy Jethro and I camped overnight at Whitefish Point. We woke up early the next morning. It was quite cool. But it was a very beautiful, sunny morning. We hoisted the sails and shoved off.

The breeze was light, but steady. The wind took us across the shipping channel toward Ile Parisienne. We were cruising at a speed of about 10 knots. As we approached the island, we changed our coarse a bit. We angled a few degrees farther west toward Batchawana Bay. By this time, the sun had risen high in the sky and warmed things up nicely. The Canadian shoreline looks so majestic from out on Lake Superior. It is really indescribable—the beauty of Lake Superior met by rolling mountains, islands and bays.

As we approached the mainland, we sailed toward an island. It was South Sandy Island. We decided to stop there. Finding a smooth spot on the beach around a point, we pulled up on shore. The sun was hot. So we both took our snorkels and masks and swam out to explore the waters around the island. But even on hot days, you don't stay long in Lake Superior's waters. Once we got out, we warmed up on the shore. We ate from the many wild sugarplum trees we found along the shore.

We met a teenage couple and the guy's younger sister who had canoed to the island from the mainland. After a brief visit, we loaded our gear and shoved off. By this time, the winds were quite a bit stronger which made good sailing for us. But we were concerned for the Canadians in the canoe. We made a pass back by them to make sure they were all right before sailing to Batchawana Island.

Reaching the island, we pulled up for a brief stop to stretch our legs. We found the remains of a hastily built log shelter there—evidence of some human presence. Leaving from there, we sailed through the west channel past the Batchawana River. We were looking for the mouth of the Chippewa River. When we thought we were near it, we pulled up on shore near some cabins and asked directions. Some people there had a small sailboat. They were very interested to hear that we had just sailed from Whitefish Point.

Launching again was more difficult now because the wind and waves were quite strong. But they pushed us quickly to the mouth of the Chippewa River. With the winds behind us, we sailed up the river. We drew a lot of attention from bystanders on shore as they stood near their cabins. We landed the boat at a point about as far upstream as was navigable. We pulled up behind a restaurant. Securing the boat, we went into the restaurant and had dinner. We made a phone call to the U.S. and found out that my brother had left early from camp and was already back at home. Disappointed, Jethro and I decided to hitchhike into Sault Ste. Marie. There we sat alongside the road in a foreign country with a boat motor, sails and our gear and our thumbs out trying to hitch a ride.

"Another fine mess you got us into, Gilligan," Jethro said.

"Oh well, that's just the way it goes," I replied.

After many cars, trucks and vans had passed, a couple with a small child stopped to give us a ride. We loaded our stuff in the back of the truck. But only one of us could ride in the already crowded cab. So being "noble", I volunteered Jethro to ride in the back. When we arrived in Sault Ste. Marie. We stayed in a motel and we made arrangements for my son Caleb to come and pick us up the next morning.

It would be several weeks before I could arrange any more time off work. The weather window of opportunity for a circumnavigation had passed. So by this time, I had resigned myself to the fact that I would have to wait until the following summer to try again. But I also determined that nothing would get in my way. I scrapped my original plan and decided that I would take the time to do the entire trip all at once.

CHAPTER 9
PIRATES

It was a sunny morning, already into September. Jethro, his son Kurt, 7, and I headed up to Canada to bring the boat back. We planned to find the boat at the restaurant. Then, since it was such a nice day, we wanted to take it out sailing one last time before storing it for the winter. But when we arrived at the restaurant, it had closed. We walked down behind the building. I couldn't see the boat.

"The boat is gone," I said, looking up and down the river.

"Do you think someone stole it?' Jethro asked.

"It sure looks that way. So many people had seen us come up the river, perhaps someone had seen the boat go down the river."

I began walking down river. I knocked on doors asking if anyone had seen anything. I talked with one young couple that lived along the shore. They suggested that I talk with the woman who owned the Whispering Pines Resort farther downstream. They said she knew everything that happened around there. They said she even knew when someone else's dog craps in her yard.

So off we went to talk with her. The lady said she hadn't seen anything. She told us that the restaurant had been repossessed for the third or fourth time. She said it appeared that the woman who owned it made a livelihood foreclosing on the owners had closed the restaurant. The lady talking to us said we should have left the boat on her property. She then said that the woman we were looking for lived in Sault Ste. Marie. She looked up her phone number for us. She also mentioned that the woman owned a cabin around the point and told us where it was. We thanked her.

Jethro, Kurt and I headed off to try to find this woman's cabin. We arrived in the area where we thought the cabin would be. I began to doubt whether I would ever see my boat again. We asked around at one or two other places. We were trying to pinpoint the location of the cabin. We thought we were in the right neighborhood. Finally, driving down a long driveway, we came to a cabin. An old Frenchman appeared near the building. I got out to talk with him. I told him that we had sailed the boat across Lake Superior and had left it behind the restaurant. I described the boat and told him we were looking for this woman's cabin.

After a brief moment, he asked me, "Is the boat blue?"

"Yes."

"Is that it over there?"

I looked across a small field toward the next cabin. There was a boat partly covered with a tarp. The mast was off. But still, it was unmistakable. My heart leapt for joy.

"That's it!"

There it was. The registration number had been scraped off and the boat was hidden in a backyard. I was eager to take the boat and get home. The old Frenchman was a little unsure. He said he thought he should call the woman. Perhaps he was wondering if our story was true. We went inside and he called her on the phone. After a few words, he handed me the phone. The woman on the other end told me in a nasty tone that I owed her money for storing my boat. I tried to be respectable and I generously offered her $50. I did this even though I thought that they were pirates. She said her son worked hard to get the boat there and store it. She said she wanted $200 before I could take it. She said she didn't have time to come out to the cabin today.

Then I asked her why the registration numbers were scraped off if she was storing the boat. If she was storing the boat for me, you'd think they would have tried to contact the owner. She denied any knowledge of registration numbers. As I hung up the phone I declared loudly, "What a bitch!"

A bit bewildered at the turn of events, the older gentleman and I stepped outside. As I wondered what my next move would be, I looked out across the field. There was Jethro already backed up to the boat with the trailer. He was tying the mast on top of his van. This gave me more courage. So as I started back toward the boat, I said to the Frenchman, "You can call the police or whatever you want to do, but I'm taking the boat with me."

He just shrugged and gave me a bewildered look. I walked off. When I got to the boat, I told Jethro what had happened. I said that the quicker we could get the boat out of the yard, the better.

"You know that possession is nine-tenths of the law," I said. "And after all, it was my boat."

There was a large chain holding the boat. Fortunately, Jethro had a hacksaw. So I worked on the chain while he secured the boat to the trailer. Within minutes, we were heading out of the long driveway. We were hoping the police wouldn't show up before we got out of the yard. With the wings on the boat it was about 12 feet wide. We had to stop because there were some large maple trees along the driveway. The opening was too narrow to get the boat through.

Quickly, we jumped out of the van and attempted to pull off one of the wings, then the other. They wouldn't come off. So there we were, in a foreign country, stealing our own boat. We were expecting the police to arrive at any moment. Worse, we couldn't get the boat out of the driveway! Finally, we were able to lift the back end of the trailer just enough to slide the back end over. This allowed the right amount of room to get the trailer between the trees.

I told Jethro, "If we can make it out of the yard with the boat, since it's my own boat, it will be a civil matter, not a criminal matter. And if the woman that was demanding $200 for storage had a complaint she should have taken it to Small Claims Court. We would have a counter complaint that she would owe us over $200 for new registration numbers and a new paint job for the place where my numbers had been scraped off."

After what seemed like an eternity, we finally made it to the main highway. Rather than driving directly down the highway to Sault Ste. Marie, we turned west and crossed the Chippewa River. We headed back up the back road toward my brother's camp. We did this to try to avoid the police. We thought they surely would be coming up the highway, looking for us.

Even though we had a good story for answering the police, we would rather avoid any confrontations with the law. After all, I hadn't cleared customs with the boat when we had come across Lake Superior. So this whole thing could potentially run into a lot of red tape. We wanted to avoid all of it.

The farther off the highway and down the back road we went, the more relieved I felt. After driving a ways, we pulled over and we worked on taking off the wings. We were able to remove them. This brought the width of the boat trailer to within legal size limits for roads. We also secured the boat to the trailer tighter than it had been during our rather hasty exit.

We soon met some of my brother's friends who were coming from their camp. They told us that my brother wasn't up at his place this weekend. So we headed back for Sault Ste. Marie. Would the police stop us? Would we be hassled at customs when we crossed the border?

After making it through town and to the border, we stopped at the customs booth. The customs agent asked us a few questions. Then he motioned us through the border. We were hoping he wouldn't ask too many questions about the boat, especially why there were no registration numbers. We were hoping he wouldn't notice. We drove ahead and we didn't stop until we had the boat back safe at home in my yard.

So ended the summer and the sailing season. Again, I did not make my trip. But, this left me more determined than ever to plan better and to set aside enough time next summer to make the trip around Lake Superior.

CHAPTER 10
THE TRIP

The following summer found me busier than ever between work, family and home. It seemed I didn't have a moment of spare time. It was already July 10. I hadn't even been out on my boat yet. Naomi was the only one of my three children left at home. She decided she would make the trip around Superior with me.

We were frantically packing and making last minute preparations. Jethro came up to Munising Bay. He helped me set up the boat the night before we were to leave. That's when we discovered that the control ropes, jib sheets and headgear were missing. The thieves who tried to steal my boat the year before must still have these items. So instead of leaving the next morning as planned, I had to run down to Jethro's place and borrow the headgear off his boat. Luckily, his was the same as mine. To do this took another three hours. So by the time we got the boat packed and ready to go, it was 5 p.m. Finally, Naomi and I were ready to leave. My fiancé Dori and her two children were there to see us off. We waived goodbye as we sailed away.

Dad and I were planning to start the trip at 9 a.m., but as can be expected, things didn't work out as planned. Dad had to run down to Fayette to get a part for the boat. Then we spent time packing and dawdling until late in the afternoon. I stopped and said goodbye to Sarah and Tim, and finally Dori, Caleb and Alana saw us off from the mouth of the Anna River. Strong winds helped us reach Grand Marais just after sundown. The waves weren't very big and the weather alternated between sunshine and clouds.

—Naomi's Diary [Editor's Note: This is the first in several entries from Naomi's travel diary that will be included in this text. The entries will appear in italicized type.]

Would we make it? What perils and adventures would lie ahead? Could I really afford to take the time off? These were all questions that were going through my mind as Naomi and I waved goodbye and sailed into the distance.

We moved slowly out of Munising Bay. We could see Grand Island to our left and the old East Channel Lighthouse standing guard on its banks. The lighthouse is a historic landmark that was built in 1872. The following summer, I would hold a concert to raise money to help save the lighthouse from the eroding waves of Lake Superior.

Our sails were full as a southwest wind pushed us steadily along. To our right was Miners Castle and the beautiful Pictured Rocks National Lakeshore. The nation's first national lakeshore surely is a jewel in the crown of Lake Superior. The sheer sandstone cliffs, with their magical colors reflecting on the blue-green waters of Lake Superior, are one reason thousands of visitors take the tour boat cruises each year. Boaters of all kinds cruise the lakeshore to view these natural wonders.

We sailed on past Portal Rock with its stone archway. It is said that in the 1800s, there was another arch there that was large enough for a schooner to sail through. Erosion would eventually leave only the existing arch, which is smaller, but still majestic.

Lacking a natural harbor for safety, one of the most tragic early shipwrecks on Lake Superior took place here along the Pictured Rocks. The mishap occurred in 1856. The sidewheel steamer *Superior*, under Capt. Hiram Jones, was caught in a storm blowing out of the northwest. The boat almost made it to the shelter of Grand Island. But the ship lost its rudder and smokestack in high seas. The captain ordered the anchors dropped. But the chains broke, leaving the boat and its crew to be smashed to bits on the Pictured Rocks Cliffs, just west of Cascade Falls. Of the 66 crewmen aboard, only 18 bedraggled survivors made it to shore. Capt. Jones was last seen struggling to make it up onto the rocks. He was washed off by huge waves and was last seen in his beaver skin coat before he disappeared into the waves.

An epic tale of survival would follow. The first mate and the engineer patched a lifeboat they found washed ashore. The two men, with a few others, would make it to Grand Island, to a trader's cabin. While the others trudged through the forest on foot to be picked up later, two more sailors would die of exposure. This was the worst loss of life attributed to shipwrecks on Lake Superior up to that time.

The wind pushed us east past the Pictured Rocks, along Twelvemile Beach. We could see the Au Sable Point Lighthouse tower. Its beam of light alerts ships to the treacherous Au Sable Reef.

We passed Sable Point Lighthouse on the way here. The water was indescribably purple dabbed with mercury silver and liquid lead. The clouds were a moody blue gray with a bright blue sky peeking through the cracks. And Sable Point stood proud and white contrasting with the dark trees its white tower looking rose-colored. Beyond us stood the great dunes looking white and purple against the dark blue sky.

I think God is blessing this trip. Before we left, we asked him to be with us and we read the sailor's psalm (Psalm 107). I hope he continues to bless.

We are camped on the beach below the campground. I've written too much. I'm going to bed.

The reef had often been the scene of shipwrecks and survival struggles. The lonely lighthouses and keeper's quarters on the Great Lakes were many times used to offer refuge to storm-tossed shipwreck survivors.

Sailing on past the lighthouse, the beautiful Grand Sable Dunes stretched for miles before us. Their sands piled high, they reflected in the golden sunset. No wonder the Native Americans gathered here to fast and pray to the Great Spirit. You can't help but be awe-inspired by the majestic beauty of the dunes.

It was along these shores, from the great dunes to Grand Island, that the tales of the legendary Indian Hiawatha are said to have been handed down. Henry Schoolcraft, U.S. Indian agent, and Lewis Cass, who later would become governor of Michigan Territory, stopped at Grand Island in 1820. It is said that Schoolcraft, while on a westward expedition to find the source of the Mississippi River, was surprised to find no Indian settlement on Grand Island. To his knowledge, there had been a sizeable band of Ojibway Indians living there.

The mainland Indians told him there was an Indian living on Trout Bay. They said he could tell the story of what became of the Grand Island Ojibway band. Cass and Schoolcraft dispatched a canoe and brought back the Indian called Powers of the Air. He seems to have been a "Last of the Mohicans" type of Indian for the Grand Island Band of Ojibways. He was able to tell Schoolcraft the story of how the island band was forced to join a war party from the mainland. They had to fight the Sioux who lived to the west. The Grand Islanders thought war was senseless and did not care to join in. But when threatened with attack from the mainland Ojibways, they finally agreed. But they lost all of their men. Only Powers of the Air escaped. Being the youngest and fastest runner of the band, he was urged by the others to make a break for it and get away.

This story and many other Native American legends were told to Schoolcraft. He wrote them down and would later loan his material to a man named Henry Wadsworth Longfellow. Longfellow then wrote *The Song of Hiawatha* based on some of these stories. Schoolcraft and Cass continued on their voyage only to be caught in a sudden storm, pulling in at the sands of AuTrain, they waited out the storm. While they were there, one of the party members was so impressed with Powers of the Air he carved a likeness of his face in the rock along the shore, and it's still there to this day! Loren Graham's book *A Face in the Rock* chronicles this story in detail. The story also inspired me to write this song:

FACE ON THE ROCK

Face on the rock speak to me
Tell me a tale of how it used to be
On your island Grand, you'd run along the sand

He was born long ago to an island band of the Ojibways, Ojibways
Beneath the stars in his mother's arms
She told him tales, sang him songs of days gone by
When she heard him cry

But Powers of the Air he don't live there no more
He don't run along the shore
So take me back home, back home to yesterday-hey-hey
Take me back home, back home to yesterday

The ways of peace were always known
But now the talk of war was heard
On our island home I was almost grown
Twelve brave men would sail away
But only one returned again
Another day, another day

All tribes of men should live as one

Beneath the stars and the setting sun
So take me back home, back home to yesterday-hey-hey
Take me back home, back home to yesterday

The years would pass, the white man came
Life would never be the same
On our island home I was all alone

In my dreams, the beaver returned
The sound of song and laughter
Was heard again, was heard again

Tonight, I'll walk a path of the Milky Way
Gather me there with my family
Take me back home, back home to yesterday—hey—hey
Take me back home, back home to yesterday

Take me back home to my island Grand, where I used to run along the
sand
Take me back home, back home to yesterday-hey-hey
Take me back home to yesterday

We hit some pretty strong wind passing the dunes. It made for fast sailing, but a little scary at times. I was steering the boat when we got to Grand Marais we saw a fire and pulled up to it, there were some nice people there and we ended up sitting and visiting with them half the night. They liked to sing, so we sang (of course). One of the girls had a pretty voice, kind of like Sarah McLaughlin. They invited us to breakfast tomorrow. So I will try to get their e-mail address. The one lady is kind of new age. She told stories about her fairy encounters. They seem like nice interesting people. I will never forget the sunset.

Arriving just after dark at Grand Marais we saw a campfire on the beach. Naomi and I pulled our boat up and joined a small group of people around the fire. We told them about our adventure plans of sailing around Lake Superior. We also told them that we sang Great Lakes songs. It was interesting to find out that they were also singers and musicians. I believe they called themselves "The Lakers." So we pulled out our little back-packer's guitar and sang a few songs for them. In the glow of the camp-fire, we told stories and sang songs. It was a wonderful way to start our trip around Superior.

CHAPTER 11
TROUBLE

Morning came. Naomi and I had slept under the stars in our sleeping bags. We awoke to the lapping of the waves on the shore. There is nothing I have ever experienced like camping on the Lake Superior shore. We crawled out of our sleeping bags and decided to walk to the store to buy a couple of last minute things we needed. We would be sailing into some remote areas where it would be days, or weeks, before we'd have any chance of re-supplying.

We had been invited to eat breakfast with the folks we had met the night before. So on our way back to the boat, we stopped by their campsite. But we found them still asleep. Naomi and I decided it was time to get moving. The southwest wind continued to blow as it had the day before, pushing us past the old Grand Marais Coast Guard Station. I knew the building well. My son Caleb and I had repainted it the summer before. While working there, we learned many stories of the courage and valor of the lifesaving crews.

As Naomi and I sailed by the Grand Marais Harbor entrance and headed east, I recalled the story of the *Parker* for her. They say the ship was pounded by a southwest wind back in 1907. The old wooden steamer began to sink while it was heading for shore. The captain blew the ship's whistle, which alerted the Grand Marais lifesaving crew. After a tiring 50-minute row, the lifesavers reached the vessel.

Not able to carry all 17 of her crewmen, the *Parker's* yawl was launched and eight of her crew followed. The ship sank soon afterward. After several hours of rowing against the wind and waves, the two boats neared the harbor. Two tugs picked up the tired rowers and towed them in to shore.

Naomi and I sailed east. The southwest wind was quite strong and seemed to be getting stronger. We sailed past the spot where Caleb and I had stopped to repair the damaged jib the year before. Naomi and I made good time. When we reached the Two-hearted River, we decided to pull in and take a little break. As we were eating lunch, I noticed a sailboat about a half-mile offshore. The occupants of the boat seemed to be having difficulty. It looked as though they had lowered the sail and were trying to start their motor. But they were stuck in the high wind and waves. As I was watching them, their situation seemed to be getting worse. I ran over to the boat and got my radio. I had a small hand-held unit. I turned it on. I watched the boaters for a few more minutes. Then I heard the harbormaster of the Little Lake Marina trying to reach the sailboat on the radio. The marina was a located a mile or two away from us. I spoke to the harbormaster briefly and told him I had been watching the boaters too. He said he could go out and assist them in his Boston whaler powerboat, which is a very seaworthy craft.

The harbormaster had been trying to contact the boat for a while. But there had been no response. We watched the boaters for a while longer. Apparently, they got their motor working and started making some headway going west.

I was standing at the very spot where one of the old lifesaving stations along the Shipwreck Coast had been standing in 1875. There were four stations in all. They were located at Vermilion Point, Crisp Point, Two-hearted River and Muskallonge Lake at Deer Park. How many times had the brave men here witnessed ships in distress? In the early days of shipping on the lake, there were so many shipwrecks along this coast that these four manned lifesaving stations were built about 10 miles apart. History has largely forgotten these "storm warriors," which was the nickname given these members of the U.S. Lifesaving Service. A 24-hour beach patrol would walk the shore continuously. They would meet between stations and exchange a token, proving they had made their rounds. If they should see a ship too close to shore, or in danger, they would light a flare to warn them of danger or to acknowledge their distress. How many times had they launched their surfboats to row through breaking waves to rescue ship's crews? I felt their awesome responsibility for a few minutes while I stood there.

Today was not a good day for me. It was one of those days where nothing goes right. The windbreaker Daddy got me blew off the boat, which perturbed me greatly because I really, really liked it. The flies were terrible and ate me up. And when we finally made camp I lost my glasses. So I'm really in a bad mood. I need to pray about this because I don't want to be like the children of Israel (complaining).

As far as progress goes, we did pretty good. We ate breakfast at the diner in Grand Marais. It was a really cool restaurant and I had some

French toast. We pulled out of Grand Marais about 10 a.m. and got to Whitefish Point about sunset. On our first stretch, the waves and wind were erratic and puffy. But then after we stopped at the mouth of the Two-Hearted River, things calmed down a little.

The wind blew more steady and the waves turned into huge rollers. It was a long boring stretch between Grand Marais and Whitefish Point.

When Naomi and I finished our lunch, we set sail again. By now, the waves were 4 to 5 feet high. The winds were quite strong. So we had reefed the mainsail. Naomi and I launched the boat, sailing past Little Lake toward Whitefish Point. With the lake getting rougher, we tried to stay a bit closer to land. Unfortunately, we had trouble on the other side of Little Lake. We were trying to make it around a small point of land when our rudders hit bottom. This caused them to kick up, making it very difficult to steer.

In the heavy seas and strong winds, all I could do was run the boat up onto the shore. Fortunately, this is one of the best features of a catamaran—the ability to beach. With some difficulty, we pulled the boat up. There we were on a narrow strip of beach right near the pounding surf. We did not want to stay there. We set our sails to tack into the wind and decided to launch out into the breakers. If we got caught sideways in these waves, the boat would surely be pounded to pieces. Would we make it back to deep water? Or would this be the end of our trip?

The wind caught our sail and pulled us through the breakers and finally into deep water where I could lock my rudders down. We cleared the point and we were on our way. We made good time with following seas, stayed farther out from shore and we had no more problems that day.

Crips Point Lighthouse was a welcome sight with its lone tower, contrasting boldy against the dark sky.

We sailed past the old Vermilion Point Lifesaving Station and on to Whitefish Point. As we got closer to Whitefish Bay, we could see the lighthouse tower reflecting in the evening sun. The winds were dying down and the waves were beginning to calm. We could now relax a bit.

With Whitefish Point now in sight and the seas running a bit more calmly, I was able to tell Naomi of another interesting story.

"It happened right out there," I said, pointing. "About a mile and a half offshore, it was the strange story of a shipwreck, believe it or not."

The crew all got off in the lifeboats and the captain went down with his ship. But the captain was the only one who survived.

"How could that be," Naomi asked?

Well it happened like this, there was another November storm in 1919. The 186-foot wooden steamer—the *Myron*—was towing another ship called the *Miztec*. But the pounding of the waves caused the ship to leak badly. Hoping to make it around the point, Captain Neal of the *Myron* dropped his towline and ran for shelter. But the ship was in serious trouble. A passing ore carrier called the *Adriatic*, noticing the ship was in trouble, pulled alongside to protect her as the *Myron* desperately tried to reach safety.

The Vermilion Point Coat Guard sailors also noticed the ship's plight and launched their lifeboat through the terrible surf. Only a mile and a half form the point, the little ship gave up. As the *Myron* began to sink, her crew climbed into the lifeboats. But Captain Neal decided to go down with his beloved ship.

Meanwhile, the men in the lifeboats were in a desperate situation. The deckload of lumber now awash in the pounding seas hammered the lifeboats. The *Adriatic* made several attempts to rescue. But when the big ship began to hit bottom, the captain retreated her to deeper water.

Another ship, the 520-foot *H.P. McIntosh* actually drew close enough to throw lifelines to the survivors. But weakened by the freezing cold, they were unable to save themselves. The captain of the *McIntosh,* fearing for his own ship and crew, had to pull away. The Coast Guard crew, likewise, was unable to penetrate the pounding debris. All 16 crewmen perished.

Meanwhile, Captain Neal had gone down with his ship. But as the ship sank, the pilothouse popped off and Captain Neal climbed onto the roof of what had become a makeshift raft. For 20 miserable long hours he drifted in the storm.

The next day, the captain of the *W.C. Franz* spotted a body on some wreckage. He turned his ship to pick up the body. To his surprise, he saw the body move. Captain Neal was rescued, barely alive. His body was some 20 miles from the wreck, but he recovered and was actually the only member of the ship's crew who survived.

"Wow! That's a great story," Naomi said.

We sailed for the shore and pulled the boat up onto the beach near the lighthouse. Naomi and I unloaded our gear and set up camp. It was a beautiful evening. The sun setting over the big lake and the distant mountains on the Canadian shore left a lasting impression of the awesome beauty of Lake Superior.

We stopped twice today after the Two-Heart before reaching here. Hopefully, God will bless again tomorrow. It was another beautiful red sunset again tonight and there was a freighter inching its way across the horizon. We had macaroni and cheese for supper. Yummy.

CHAPTER 12
CANADA

Today finds me in much better spirits. We pulled out of Whitefish Point around 8 a.m. and headed straight across the tail of the lake to Batchawana Bay. Before we left, I found my glasses, which made me very happy. The lake is very calm. We had to motor all the way across.

The next morning, Naomi and I awoke to a beautiful sight. There was a light fog over the water. I was eager to sail for the Canadian shore. To cut straight across the bay would save us three or four days travel. But, crossing the 20 to 25 miles to the other shore could become treacherous if the wind should pick up. Even large freighters have been sunk by the wind, waves and storms on the lake.

One of the most famous shipwrecks of the area was that of the 729-foot *Edmund Fitzgerald*, which sank only about 15 miles from the spot we were launching from. What chance would a 16-foot sailboat have? Lost in a storm on Nov. 10, 1975, the *Fitzgerald* has become the flagship of Great Lakes shipwrecks. It reminds all sailors of the awesome power of these inland seas.

But today, the weather reports sounded as good as we could hope for. We launched the boat in light winds and sailed across one of the largest stretches of open water we would encounter during the entire trip. The Whitefish Point Lighthouse tower grew smaller and smaller. That light-house has witnessed perhaps more shipwreck tragedies than any other place in the world.

As we sailed on, the winds grew even lighter. I told Naomi that I'd start the boat motor. Our 3-horsepower Tanaka could push us along in calm weather at a pace of about 5 ? or 6 miles per hour. The motor helped us move toward the Canadian shore. The light fog prevented us from seeing the other shore. So we sailed by compass and a hand-held global positioning satellite system. This unit was very helpful. The course we were on took us across one of the busiest shipping channels in the world. We saw freighters in the distance. We figured they were so far away we would be across the shipping channel and in safe waters by the time any of the ships came close to us. We were wrong. Let me tell you, those ships are moving a lot faster than they look. Before we knew it, there was a large down bound freighter moving up on us. I was beginning to wonder if my calculations were correct. The ship got closer. I started to get nervous.

"I wonder if they can even see us on their radar?" I said.

I had Naomi pull out our small hand-held radio. She handed it to me. I turned to what I thought was the proper channel and said, "Hailing the freighter off Whitefish Point."

I repeated the message: "Hailing the freighter off Whitefish Point." No response.

"That freighter is getting awfully close," I said.

The thing was so big. I couldn't tell exactly which angle the ship was taking as it moved. Should I continue on my same course? Should I turn around and try to go back? Does he see me? If he does see me, is he changing his course so that if I change mine he might be running right over us? With some misgiving, I turned the boat around. I was hoping that I was making the right decision. I can understand now why there were so many fatal shipwrecks from collisions off Whitefish Point.

Once such horrible accident took place on Aug. 20, 1920. The 429-foot down bound *Superior City* and the up bound *Willis L. King* came together with a terrible crash. There was confusion between the two vessels as to which side they were to pass. At the last minute, the *Superior City* turned across the *King's* bow. The ship struck with an awful crash. The crew of the *Superior City* rushed desperately to leave their sinking steamer. But for most of the sailors time had already run out. It was too late to launch the lifeboats. Water flooded into the boiler room, which caused an explosion. The blast killed nearly all the crew who were directly above the engine room. These were the sailors who had been preparing the lifeboats. The explosion knocked four crewmen clear of the wreck. The remaining 29 went down with the ship in about two minutes time.

I would say that is about how close we came to being run over by this freighter. If we had stayed our intended course, we would have struck the huge ship in about two minutes time. The freighter cruised past us larger than life. I was relieved to see that I had made the right decision. I was lucky. There were others who were not. Naomi and I had begun the day with a prayer that God would give us safe travel. This time, he surely had.

We had all we could do to scramble out of the path of an oncoming freighter. It passed very close to us. It was beautiful watching it go by through the early morning mist. I'd never seen one so close under full steam. It was interesting. I could see an officer riding his round on a bike and I could picture in my mind the men sitting, drinking their coffee and getting the feel of the morning.

With the freighter incident behind us now, we motored toward the Canadian shore. The fog seemed to get thicker as the day went on. When you can't see where you're going it can be very frustrating. Does this compass work right? Are we going the right way? Shouldn't we be there by now? These were some of the questions I had in my mind. All we could do was trust our instruments.

The passage seemed to last forever. The water stretched on and on for what seemed like eternity and a haze obscured the shore. It felt like I was going crazy. Thoughts kept popping into my head like what if we were heading toward the middle of the lake? And what if the motor quits in the middle of a shipping route?

I wanted to see land so badly that my mind started playing tricks on me and I was seeing land where there was no land. This trip is bad for my teeth. I grind them at least three times a day.

Sometime around noon, we spotted the outline of the mountainous Canadian shore. What a welcome sight. "We made it Naomi, across some of the most dangerous waters in the world!"

CHAPTER 13

THE CANADIAN SHORE

After what seemed to be an eternity of following our compass through the fog, we finally spotted the Canadian shoreline. Like a giant peeking over the top of a fence, the mountaintops of Corbeil Point welcomed us through the fog. By this time, the waters had calmed and were nearly as smooth as glass. We motored on using the outboard,. We checked our speed and our progress on our handheld GPS unit.

With the dangerous open water crossing behind us, and the beauty of the Canadian shore drifting past at 5½ miles per hour, I now truly began to relax and enjoy the trip. A feeling of elation enveloped us. The warm sunlight melted away the fog. The beauty of the massive granite rock mountains reaching down to the deep, clear waters of Lake Superior soothed all thoughts of any storms on the lake, past or future. They were momentarily forgotten.

Canada was immediately beautiful and has not ceased to awe me yet. We stopped at a little fishery out of Batchawana Bay. The lake stayed flat all day. But we motored to the Montreal River. We saw a lot of loons and a lot of awesome scenery.

Across Batchawana Bay and on toward Coppermine Point, we glided across the calm waters, taking in the unfolding beauty all around us. Coppermine Point, on a calm day, is a reminder that not all shipwrecks on the Great Lakes were caused by collisions or heavy seas. Sometimes, fire would destroy vessels on the lakes.

A spectacular fire off Coppermine Point, on the night of June 26, 1907 claimed the 26-year-old wooden Canadian steamer *Batchawana*, just a few miles from Batchawana Bay. Down bound with a load of iron ore from Fort William to the Algoma Steel Company in Sault Ste. Marie, Ont., the 209-foot, 674-ton vessel somehow caught fire. The ship was quickly engulfed in flames. The crew took to the lifeboats and was saved. But their ship had made her last trip.

Rounding Coppermine Point, we looked out on the lake and saw the form of a fish tug out in the distance. As we traveled on, we could see that both of us were headed in the same direction. I smiled and turned to Naomi.

I pointed to the fish tug and said, "It looks like we'll be having fresh fish for supper tonight."

"Can you do that? Buy fish right off their boat?"

"Of course. The fishermen can eliminate the middleman. We can get fresh fish."

So both of our boats cruised toward the small harbor, which was protected by some rocky islands. The tug reached the harbor ahead of us. They had already tied up and unloaded. The harbor was rather quiet when we pulled up the boat. It was nice to stretch our legs a little. It was already early afternoon.

We made our way into the fish house and were greeted by a woman behind a counter. We told her about our trip and that we would like to buy some fish. She weighed some trout and smoked whitefish. She packed it in ice and a cardboard box. We strapped the fish onto our boat, shoved off and we were on our way.

Later that fall at Whitefish Point, one of the fishermen from the tug was at the Edmund Fitzgerald memorial service. The service is held each Nov. 10 as a reminder of the terrible storm that sank the great freighter and her crew. The fisherman told those gathered how on the night of the storm, the water along the shore here was 15 feet higher than normal. He also said that a lot of wreckage from the Fitzgerald was washed ashore near his fishery, including a lifeboat from the Fitzgerald.

Naomi and I continued west along the rocky Canadian coast. It was one of the best days of my life. We motored along at top speeds of 6 mph. over waters that looked just like glass. The water was so clear and pure we could see the boulders and crevices below us to 30 feet deep. Naomi lay sprawled out on one of the bows of the boat, while I leaned back against the side stays and took in the warmth of the sun. There are not many days like this on Lake Superior. So when they come along, enjoy them.

Up until this point, I still had doubts about the trip. I kept asking myself questions. Am I crazy taking this much time off work? Is it foolhardy to attempt such a voyage? Will we make it all the way around this time? But when the weather is fine and the awesome beauty of the rugged shoreline is drifting by you have no doubts. The answer is yes, yes, yes, and more than yes—this was the right thing to do. It was the trip of a lifetime. There would be days ahead when I would ask myself these questions again. But for today, we just sat back and enjoyed ourselves.

By late afternoon, we were approaching the mouth of the Montreal River. So we pulled up at the mouth in front of a small resort. Our 2½-gallon supply of gasoline was getting rather low from running our motor all day. We walked up to the resort. It consisted of a few small cabins. We found the office and went inside.

The office served as a small store for the visitors at the resort. The manager was a friendly Canadian who said he was filling in for his brother who was away. When we asked about gasoline, he said they didn't have gas. But he said there was a place a few miles up the road. He said he would give us a ride over there and back. So we enjoyed the conversation as well as the ride. This was the kind of nice people we met along our way. They made the trip more enjoyable.

Back at the river mouth, we launched the boat. We could see Montreal Island in the distance. The golden sun of late afternoon made everything around appear even more beautiful. Setting our course for the island, we planned to camp there that night.

The lake was as smooth as glass again. The light reflecting from its surface looked like mother of pearl. This was a rare day indeed. So unlike the day in May 1924 when the up bound steamer *Orinoco*, with the barge *Chieftain* in tow, encountered 60 mph. winds and sub-freezing temperatures. The ship began leaking badly. Captain Anthony Lawrence ordered the towline dropped. Later, he ordered 19 of his men into the lifeboats while he and two others remained on board in an attempt to nurse the vessel to shore. As the crew in the lifeboats struggled to reach Montreal Island, they watched their 295-foot ship plunge to the bottom of the lake. The brave captain, the chief engineer and the wheelsman all went down with the ship. The men in the lifeboats were having a desperate struggle to survive. Two of the men died of exposure. Fortunately, the tug *Gargantua* happened to be in the area. The tug picked up the 17 men who had survived. They were alive, in part, due to the heroism of the three who had gone down with the ship. The *Gargantua* was able to make it to the lee of Montreal Island and anchor safely.

There is a resort we stopped at on the Montreal River. I called Mommy. We bought some food, got some gas. Then we headed out to Montreal Island.

CHAPTER 14
ATTACKED

As we neared the island, the sun was getting low in the sky. Looking for a suitable place to land, we found a sand bar protruding from the shore and pulled up in a small cove. It looked like an ideal spot to camp. We were hungry as bears after hibernating. So immediately, we began to gather wood for a campfire. At last, we would be able to cook our fish.

One of the tricks to cooking on an open fire is to not build too big a fire. A small fire is much easier to control. When our fire had burned down a bit, I placed our small grill over the fire. I put the lake trout on the grill, skin side down. This allowed the natural fats and oils of the fish to cook off. This also released the skin from the fish. This has become one of my favorite ways to cook fish. I sprinkle some Lipton onion soup mix on the exposed surface. When the fish has cooked I take a spatula and work it between the skin and the fish. I lift the fillet, leaving the skin on the grill. I flip the fish over back onto the skin. Then I sprinkle a little more soup mix on the top. "M-m-m-m-m-m good."

The sun was now setting as we began to feast on our fish and other "fixins." All of a sudden we were attacked by a swarm of hungry mosquitoes that came out of the forest. By the time we had finished supper, we were totally annoyed by the persistent little pests. Quickly packing up our gear we were now in full retreat. Shoving off, I started the motor and we were off toward the mainland, a few miles off in the distance.

The island was beautiful. We ate our fish there. It was yummy. But we discovered that the island was unbearably infested with mosquitoes. So Dad and I packed up the boat hurriedly and did some night sailing. It was beautiful to see the sails silhouetted against the stars.

As it turned dark, we could see the light for Sinclair Harbor. Suddenly, the wind picked up and caught in the mainsail we still had up. Soon, we were going faster with the wind than we were with the motor, so I shut it off. A storm was moving in and the winds became stronger. They pushed us faster and faster. As we entered the harbor, it was pitch dark. We turned on our flashlight to guide us. There were a couple of large sailboats anchored in the harbor. Our boat, being under sail, had difficulty moving around them in the wind. It was quite a feat. Finally, we spotted a little area of beach and we pulled our boat up and set up the tent. No sooner were we safe inside when the storm hit. We could hear the rain pounding on our tent and the thunder crashing. But we were safe and warm in our sleeping bags.

Things got a little hairy though. We headed toward a light and it brought us into a sheltered little harbor with other boats anchored here. After crawling along the shore for a while, we finally found a place to pull up—a pebbly little beach at the back of the bay. That's where we camped. The north shore is awesome.

CHAPTER 15

MORE FISH

The next morning, we awoke to find the storm over with and the sun poking through the clouds. Some Indian fishermen were up at dawn. They were getting ready to check their nets. Their large metal boat was launched each day. They put in and were gone.

As we were eating breakfast, another fisherman came and launched his boat. After a short time, he returned. I talked with him. He said that it was too rough for him to lift his nets that day. So I helped him load his boat onto the trailer. It seemed like the old guy was missing a few of his faculties because he seemed to stumble a lot and his speech seemed a bit slurred. Although, once he got talking, he was quite knowledgeable about the area. He told us some Native American pictographs were on the rocks just around the corner. Naomi and I loaded up and set sail out of the harbor. We took a swing by the pictographs of warriors and monsters. One is said to be of Mishibishu, the great storm spirit of the lake. The creature is said to swirl his great tail in the water, churning up the lake's great storms.

Progress was slow that day. The waves were rough from the night before. But the winds weren't too strong. We sailed slowly along.

The place we camped is called Sinclair Cove. We didn't leave the cove until noon. I took a bath in the lake. We washed out a few clothes and Dad took a nap while I picked blueberries up on a cliff. When we finally left the cove, we pulled out into monstrous seas, cloudy skies, but almost no wind. That makes for bad sailing. We made it out to Lizard Island. I clung terrified to the mast the whole way. Why is it that not a day passes on this trip in which I am not afraid for my life?

We could see South Lizard Island and Rowe Island, nearby. As we past Rowe Island, a lightning storm was approaching with loud claps of thunder. So we headed for land. We saw a good spot near the mouth of Baldhead River.

We tried to stop at Lizard Island but the weather drove us away from it. The wind was light and variable so we motored it for a while until one of the monstrous waves doused our motor and it quit. So there were, stalled in the biggest waves I've ever been out in, drifting towards the rocky coastline—yet another moment of terror. I think this is going to be a spiritual journey. I'm constantly praying.

Well, finally, Dad got the motor to work and we motored to a stony beach with a river. We think it's Baldhead, but we're not sure. We put up the tent and spent the day fishing, sleeping and reading. A thunderstorm rolled by, but it wasn't very big. I hope Mommy's not freaked out that I didn't call her tonight. Just watch, the Coast Guard will be looking for us tomorrow. It's about 10 miles to Wawa from here. Hopefully, we'll make it tomorrow if conditions are right.

We saw bolts of lightning nearby as we pulled up to the shore.

We were in a bit of a hurry. We did not want to be out on the water with a 30-foot aluminum mast sticking skyward in a thunderstorm. We quickly set up our tent and grabbed our sleeping bags and went inside. By now, it was pouring down rain. So we lit our candle lantern, got some reading materials out and waited out the storm.

By the time the rain stopped, it was late afternoon. So we decided to stay the night and get an early start in the morning. A couple of hikers walked by. We talked with them briefly. They told us that this was Lake Superior Provincial Park and that we had camped near a main hiking trail. I tried my luck fishing. I cast my line out into the current, but the fish weren't in a biting kind of mood that day.

We are planning on breaking camp very early while it's still calm tomorrow. We had Rahman noodles for supper tonight (Oriental flavor). Then we sat around the fire singing songs and playing guitar. It's been a pretty good day, even though we only went about 10 miles. I hope we do better tomorrow. I was looking at the map. We still have a long ways to go. I refuse to sail in waves that big again. I'll never forget how they looked. Not like waves, but like big blue hills. I thank God once again for his protection. I just heard a loon call.

The next morning, we were up early and we packed our gear. We were soon off and running. A dense fog hung over us most of the day. The waters were a bit choppy and it was cold with a light drizzle. The winds were rather uncooperative, causing us to use the motor intermittently throughout the day.

Coasting along the shore through the Gargantua area, even in the fog, the beauty of this area was outstanding. Small islands and a bay gave us some protection from the weather. We picked our way along the coast. Each mile we went, we were more convinced that small boat travel was the way to see the rocky Canadian coast.

We broke camp very early this morning. It was an overcast day with a very heavy mist. We motored along for a good long way with a very heavy mist. Traveling a long time past some awesome country, the cliffs were massive. There were islands and bays and every now and then the fog would lift a little and give everything a soft golden hue. We were motoring along and saw a fishing boat. So we sailed up to them and bought a fish fresh off the boat. Then we pulled into a magnificent pebbly beach with enormous cliffs rising on every side and a little creek on one side.

We made our fire in a little nook in the rocks and ate our fish. Our next stop, we pulled into Old Woman Bay. Dad met a friendly photographer from down near Toronto who took Dad to get some gas and then he took pictures of us and the boat. I got kind mad at Dad because after we left Old Woman Bay I was expecting to go to town — the town of Michipicoten . But instead, he cut across the bay to go to Michipicoten Island.

Later that day, we came across some Indian fishermen pulling their nets. So I pointed to them. I said to Naomi, "It looks like we're going to have fish for supper again." She was a bit skeptical about just going over and trying to buy fish right out in the lake. But that didn't stop me. I pulled alongside them.

I asked, "How much for a fish?" I gestured the size with my hands.

There were three men, obviously of Native descent.

One yelled back, "Five bucks."

I yelled to him, "It's a deal."

I pulled up closer to their boat. Five dollars Canadian meant about three dollars U.S. So it really wasn't a bad price for a nice size lake trout. One of the men held up a trout that was still flipping its tail. I nodded in approval. In an instant, he had the fish cleaned. I gave them the five bucks and we were on our way.

Later that day, as we passed rocky cliffs along the shore, we found a small pebble beach to pull up on. A bit protected from the wind, it was a great place to have dinner. So we gathered wood for a fire and cooked the fish my favorite way—over the open fire on my grill. There is just something about cooking fresh lake trout over an open fire. Add to that being along the Canadian shore of Lake Superior. It makes you feel in harmony with nature. There was almost a feeling of elation as I cooked the fish with the rocky cliffs rising on both sides of us. The waves were lapping up on the shoreline. Surely, the Great Spirit had blessed us to be a part of this awesome place, even if it was only for a short time.

While the fish was cooking, Naomi went for a swim and got cleaned up in the lake. She has always been quite tolerant of cold water, more so than the average human being. She has been so good on this trip. She hadn't been complaining when there have been hardships. She is surely a unique child of mine whose company has made this voyage much more enjoyable.

After dinner, we sailed westward. It was early afternoon and the sun was breaking through the fog. Then, suddenly, the fog was gone and a fresh breeze picked up. It pushed us quickly along. Soon we were at Old Woman Bay, where we pulled up to the shore. This was a place where the main highway was near the lakeshore. For the first time on the Canadian shore, there were quite a few people on the beach. We befriended one curious onlooker. He was a young man from near Toronto who was pursuing a career as a professional photographer. He gave me a ride to the nearest store so I could pick up a few supplies and fill our gas can.

He had a kayak on his car. He was very interested in our trip. I told him I wrote songs about the Great Lakes. I gave him one of my cassette tapes for giving me a ride. When we returned, he took quite a few photographs of Naomi and I. I even offered to pay him a deposit for some of his pictures. But he declined. He said he would send me some when they were developed. But I have never heard from him again. I wish I would. He probably had some good photos.

In the distance, framed by the rocky cliffs on both sides of the bay, was Michipicoten Island. This mysterious island appeared to float above the surface of the water. It is said that at times the island is invisible, even on clear days. Because of this optical illusion, Native Americans believed that spirits guarded the island. Some Indians who had gone to the island to dig for copper were poisoned by copper oxide and died mysteriously while on their way back to the mainland. This added to the belief that spirits protected the island from intruders. I'm sure that the lake itself made the journey of 15 or 20 miles risky, especially in birch bark canoes. The tales of the mysterious island were too much for Naomi and I. We saw the island floating in the distance and we headed straight for it. We had to investigate.

With a fair breeze, we were on our way toward the island. We were making good time. But the waves got bigger and bigger, so big, in fact, that Naomi was praying again. I changed course for the other side of Michipicoten Harbor on the mainland.

On Dec. 3, 1906, big waves pounded the 130-foot, 980-ton steamer *Goldspie*. The ship was being damaged by the weather. Captain Harry Boult also turned toward Michipicoten Harbor, but was forced to head for Brule Bay. There, the ship ran up on a gravel beach, broadside. The waves had won out. There was no loss of life. But several of the ship's crew suffered crippling injuries from frostbite, as they walked for shelter after the accident.

Fortunately for Naomi and I, the winds calmed and then shifted from the west to the north, allowing us to head for the mouth of the University River, where we camped for the night. The beach was made up of all large cobblestones. That didn't allow us to pitch the tent anywhere. So we put the tent up on the trampoline of the catamaran and slept in comfort that night.

I've been in the wilderness for five days now, cold and wet every day, smelling like fire smoke. And all I wanted to do was to take a shower. So you can imagine that I was disappointed, especially since there isn't another town for the next hundred miles of coast.

Well anyway, I forgave him because half way across the bay we ran out of wind and had to back track and he felt really bad about it.

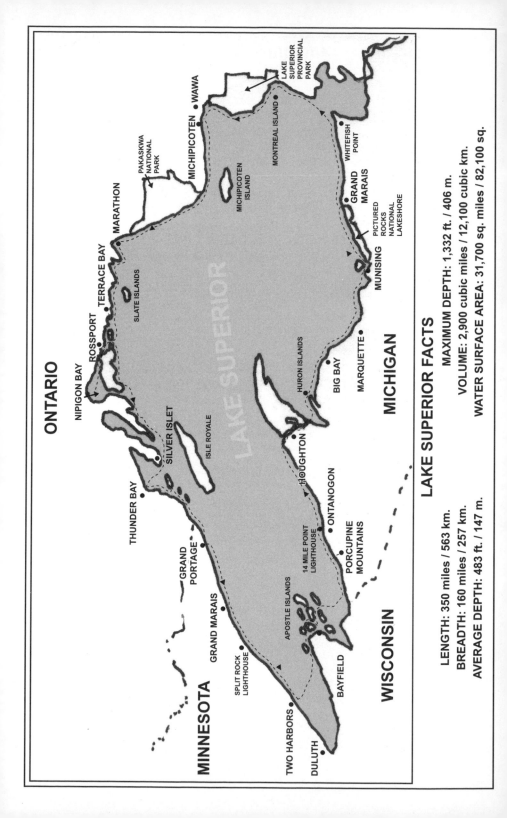

My grandparents "Caretakers" house at the Bungalow. My dog is standing on the pedestal for the old sundial, in what was once a beautiful flower garden.

My daughters Sarah and Naomi helped restore the lighthouse.

Learning to sail one of my first sailboats on Indian Lake.

Restoring Seul Choix Point Lighthouse where I wrote my first Great Lakes Song.

My son Caleb on our first attempt around the Lake at Vermillion life saving station.

Dori and her family sending us off as Naomi and I begin our journey.

Henry Ford's house at Peqaming, Michigan on the shore of Lake Superior where my Grandfather was a caretaker.

Carl and Aunt Helvi in front of my great granparents' homestead on the shore of Lake Superior along the Keweenaw Bay.

The wreck of the Myron. All of her crew escaped in the life boats while the captain went down with the ship. But strangely enough, he was the only one to survive.
Photo courtesy of Bowling Green State University.

A perfect sailing day along the Pictured Rocks.

Captain of my own ship at last.

Pulled up on the rugged and beautiful Canadian shore.

Sailing past the South Portage entry near Houghton.

Escaping a thunder storm in one of our hastily built shelters with a hot cup of mocha and a small fire.

The old life saving station at Vermillion, one of four manned life saving stations along the shipwreck coast.

When we reached the Apostle Islands winds were now behind us and the waters much warmer. Naomi and I felt like we were in the Carribean.

Naomi exploring Lamb Island on the Canadian side.

Silver Islet Mine built on a seven acre rock in Lake Superior, site of the richest silver strike in North America.
Photo credit: www.canadianheritage.ca ID #20480

Naomi on the Huron Islands at one of Lake Superior's most beautiful places.

Shipwreck of the LaFayette on the Northern Minnesota shoreline.
Photo courtesy of Western Reserve Historical Society.

High above the lake on a granite cliff is the Huron Island Lighthouse.

Canada camping on a big rock at Coldwell Harbor.

A visit to the old cemetary at Silver Islet.

1895 Moonlight and Kent washed ashore near Marquette where they spent the winter.
Photo courtesy of Superior View Photography.

Naomi and I taking it easy at Serindipity Gardens in Rossport, Ontario.

Grand Island's East Channel Lighthouse bids us goodbye as we sail out of Munising Bay and begin our journey.

Naomi takes a bath in cold Canadian waters.

The only store in the town of Silver Islet.

My darling daughter smiling for the camera.

Cooking fish over an open fire somewhere on the Canadian shore.

From left to right: Carl, Paul Johnson, Steve Johnson with the Vallhalla after another sailing season.
Photo courtesy of Steve Johnson.

Strange tidal wave like storm that hit us near Rossport.

Murray and Donna Smeltzer on their fish tug converted into a cruising yacht.

Camping along the Canadian shore.

Not far out in front of where Naomi and I pitched our tent, the 195' luxury yacht Gunilda sunk in 300' of water after striking McGarvey Shoal. Photo courtesy of Oscar Anderson.

Shaganash Island Lighthouse where we spent a night while the tornado storm had passed.

One of those rare times the lake is like glass. Naomi rides on the bow.

Naomi along the Pictured Rocks National Lakeshore.

Naomi at the old cemetery at Silver Islet.

The Gunilda: one of the finest yachts in the world, before she was lost in Lake Superior in 1911.
Photo courtesy of Bowling Green State University.

The Valhalla at her mooring on Indian Lake.
Photo courtesy of Steve Johnson.

The Apostle Islands: a sailor's paradise.

Thru the fog at Port Coldwell the old steam barge used for mining gravel for the Canadian Pacific Railway.

Fish tug in the fog along the Canadian shore.

The anchor and propeller blades from the wreck of the Kiowa, now part of a fountain in my home town of Munising. Photo courtesy of Robert and Chris Boyak.

The old house. My great grandparents' homestead along Lake Superior.

Exploring the Huron Islands.

Wind whipped and sun burned but great to be back. Dori and I attending my parents 50th Anniversary.

The beautiful shores of the Apostle Islands National Lakeshore.

CHAPTER 16
MICHIPICOTEN HARBOR

The next morning we headed out early again. This was becoming our custom because it allowed us to make some progress before the lake got too rough for travel. I was undecided as to whether we should move on or head back to Michipicoten Harbor. I could tell Naomi really had expected us to stop there. Her pouting look was enough to make me turn back.

The good news is he decided we should go to town tomorrow. When we were out in the bay, the rollers were huge, *even bigger than the ones the other day, if that's possible. But the old boat handled like a champ. Dad thought he saw a sea monster. The sunset was very beautiful and I got to watch it from the front of a sailboat while eating a cinnamon bun.*

I was wondering what my friends were doing right now. We pulled in at a little beach. It's pretty and has a river, but it's kind of buggy. We blame all the bad things lately on Michipicoten Island because it's very mysterious—an Indian legend says it's protected by evil spirits. We found a leak in our boat's hull when we made land—the curse of Michipicoten Island? Well, you decide.

It is already Day 6. We better start making some time. The name of the place we camped last night was the University River or Dog River. We left at about 10 a.m. and went to Michipicoten. The winds were pretty decent on the way there. They weren't too high. When we got to the marina, I went to take my shower but then discovered that you had to be registered for at least one night at the marina in order to take one. That was a little disappointing for me. Then we didn't think we could get a ride into Wawa to shop, but we met a nice chap who took us in. We also met some people who owned a cute little canoe and kayak outfitters' shop nearby. Dad got me a new windbreaker there. It's really nice and I like it a lot. I'm not going to let this one blow away.

I have some new e-mail addresses to add also. I'll do it later. I also called Mommy. We left later in the afternoon and the waves were rough and splashy. The wind was okay at first, then it died out and we motored it. Tonight we are on a sandy beach with many cold springs flowing out of it and big high cliffs on either side and beautiful green water. We're plan-

ning on breaking camp very early tomorrow because we need to make
some progress.

We hope to make it to the lighthouse on Otter Head Island where we
can spend the night sleeping in a building. That would be nice. We've had
the tent up on the trampoline the past two nights. It's been very comfy
though. For supper tonight we had rice with broccoli and cheese sauce.

As we sailed into the mouth of the Michipicoten River, a group of
people who were on the shore gestured to us to go on the other side of a
buoy marking the channel. They didn't know we were drawing less than
a foot of water with our boat. The wind pushed us right up the river. The
marina was upstream about a mile. That's where we pulled in.

We found out that there was no town or stores at Michipicoten Harbor.
When we asked about using the shower at the marina, the harbormaster
said we needed to be registered and pay a fee. Then he asked me if I had
cleared customs. I got a little nervous about staying there because we had
not cleared customs anywhere. So we left and went back down the river.
There was a little bay near the mouth. We pulled in there. A canoe and
kayak outfitter there was very friendly. He found us a ride to town. We
were looking for a new windbreaker jacket for Naomi because her new
one, which I had just bought for her in Grand Marais, had been lost overboard. We returned to the boat without any luck finding a jacket.

Then the kayak outfitter offered us a tour of his resort. He had a real
nice place for this kind of business. He showed great interest in Naomi
and I and our trip around the lake. He said that it had been done by canoe
and it had been done by kayak. But he said that we would be the first to
circumnavigate Superior on a beach catamaran.

In his office, they had a small store with kayak and camping supplies.
We purchased a nice red waterproof windbreaker for Naomi. She was very
happy. No pouting now.

Bidding our new friends good-bye, we sailed westward. Winds were
fair, but we were bucking big waves again and progress was slow and wet.
We camped that night on the shore along a small cove.

Leaving early to avoid high seas, we motored through calm waters in
the early morning light. It was a beautiful day. The sky was clear. The
rocky shore of the cliffs, mountains and forests gave us some majestic
scenery to enjoy. As we made our way along, we could see Michipicoten
Island in the distance. The spirits had kept us away this time. But we
swore we would return.

CHAPTER 17

OTTER HEAD ISLAND

Some of the most remote and beautiful areas on our trip lay ahead of us along the Pukaskwa Peninsula. It would be another 150 to 200 miles before we would reach any kind of civilization. I don't think there are even any roads to this area.

The morning was very calm as we glided over the smooth waters. A fish tug was sitting off in the distance. The men aboard were tending their nets. I think it was the only powerboat we saw that day. We cruised along not only enjoying the scenery above, but also the scenery below. At this point, we were probably the closest we would get to Michipicoten Island. It was very tempting to go there. But we thought we had better just stick to our agenda—sailing around the lake. We decided that at some other time we would do an "island tour," spending a summer visiting Lake Superior's great islands.

Suddenly, we felt a great jolt. Instantly, we were almost completely out of the water. I quickly shut off the motor. We were stopped dead on top of a giant round-topped boulder. The rock was sitting just below the surface. We were within sight of two shipwrecks that lay at the northwest tip of Michipicoten Island. Both of those ships had run aground there. Although, unlike us, the *Chicago* had been blown completely across the lake in a 1929 October storm. With 30-foot waves, the 324-foot steel-hulled steamer's crew made it safely to shore. Not more than a mile from that wreckage sat the 205-foot *Strathmore*. That ship struck bottom in a severe storm on Nov. 1, 1924. The ship had been down bound with a load of grain. Her crew also made it to safety before the ship sank. Today, both ships are attractions for sport divers.

So I guess we weren't the only ones to meet misfortune here. If it had been a little bit rougher, I would have seen the waves splashing over the rock. But the calm day smoothed the waters and helped conceal the boulder. Naomi and I both got out of the boat to lighten the load. We pushed it off into deeper water. Fortunately, there was no serious damage to the boat or the motor. We were soon on our way again.

After several more miles of breathtakingly beautiful scenery, we saw four guys paddling east in two canoes. They were in a "desperate" situation. As soon as we were near enough, they flagged us down and hollered for help. They had left Marathon nine days earlier and probably had two or three more days of travel to reach Michipicoten Harbor. It seems their supply of beer had run out several days earlier. They offered us as much as $10 apiece for each beer that we could spare. But alas, we had none. So unless they met someone else with a good supply, they would have to survive on only food and water for seven days.

We started out early this morning from the little harbor about 15 miles from Michipicoten Harbor. The morning was calm and excellent for motoring. We stopped at Grangly Harbor and found some Pukaskwa Pits. The pits were dug by some ancient people for unknown reasons. They were really neat.

On we went. The wind started to pick up sometime before noon, allowing us to sail along quite nicely. But the wind soon became stronger and gusted. This kicked up waves on the lake making our travel difficult. Sometime in mid afternoon we made it to Gawley's Harbour. Naomi and I were wet and tired and we needed a break. It felt good to be in the calm of the bay.

We had taken a copy of Bonnie Dahl's *A Superior Way* along with us as a guide for our trip. The book was a cruising guide that described some of the curious Pukaskwa pits located nearby. So we stopped to explore and we also wanted to stretch our legs. After a brief search, we found the pits just as they were described in the book. There was a huge area of stones about the size of coconuts that were deposited along the lakeshore by glaciers. Then the rocks were shaped into terraces by ancient lakes or catastrophic storms. These huge areas of stone scattered along the coast of the Pukaskwa Peninsula contained pits dug into the stone. Native Americans may have dug the pits for some ceremonial purposes. These "Pukaskwas," or pits, were found at nearly every location where we found huge piles of stones. The Pukaskwa Pits gave this region its name. After we found the pits and explored the harbor, we sailed westward in strong gusting west winds. It was tough going. Tacking windward, we moved from the shelter of one point of land to another. We also would duck behind islands whenever we could.

The farther we traveled the scenery became more majestic. These beautiful places always beckoned us to stay. We could not. But we did promise to return. We traveled along Pukaskwa Provincial Park. If I had to pick out just one part of the Canadian shoreline that I favored above the rest, I think this area would be the best. Its bays and rocky cliffs, forested hills and rugged coast were a continual source of wonder to us. Just when we passed some scene we thought to be beyond compare, we would round the next bend to find a scene even more beautiful. This helped us forget the hardships and the danger we had faced earlier in the day.

When we pulled out of the harbor the winds had picked up considerably from the west to the east against so we had to tack into it until about 6 o'clock, when it started to die down. Earlier in the day, when it was calm, I saw a big fish. The clear water held us as though suspended. You could see all the way down to the bottom. It was cool. It seemed like we were floating in the air.

We pulled up on a gravelly beach near the mouth of a river. Naomi and I got out of the boat to explore. Lake Superior, with her ice and wave action, had built a large bank of small stones or gravel across the mouth of the stream. A large pool had formed behind this natural dam. The gravel allowed the water to drain out slowly and yet maintain a consistent water level in the pond. The men in the canoes had described this place to us. They told us it was a good place to take a bath because it was much warmer water than that of the big lake. The pond was about 12 feet deep in the middle. It was the most natural swimming pool I had ever seen.

Naomi thought that this was the Pukaskwa River. But I didn't think it was because it was too small. After exploring a bit more, we traveled west again. We were still fighting the wind and waves until late evening. The sun was getting low and we saw a spot that looked like a good place to stop. We were both wet and tired. The place we stopped was a huge open area of small stones. We looked around and found several Pukaskwa pits. I was about to get ready to set up camp when I noticed Naomi pouting again. I had put her through a lot that day. She had changed her wet clothes several times and she had changed into the only dry thing she had left—a dress she had brought for when we got to a town.

She hardly spoke to me. But I read her thoughts. We had learned from the kayak outfitters that the lighthouse keeper's quarters at Otter Head were open to whoever wanted to use them. This meant a dry place out of the weather and a place to hang our clothes to dry. I looked at the sun over the water and said, "I bet we could make it to Otter Head by dark if we tried." Naomi packed up so quickly we were on our way in minutes.

We were under the shadow of Michipicoten Island all day almost. We pulled into camp somewhere but I had my heart set on going to Otter Head. So I pouted until Dad agreed to go.

The wind had dropped to almost nothing. The waves were no longer cresting. They had settled to smooth rolling waves. So we started the motor and headed out. Our gasoline supply was almost out. So I took the quart can of white stove gas and dumped it into our gas can. I added a little oil and shook it up.

"That will get us a little farther," I said.

As we traveled farther west, the lake grew calmer. The setting sun reflected on the water in a most beautiful way.

By this time, the winds had died down considerably and it became more calm. We were running low on gas, but we motored it anyway. It was such a beautiful ride. The sunset painted the sky red, orange, yellow and purple. The water looked like mercury and when the wind ruffled the water, it blazed with color. It looked like Lake Superior donned her finest saffron and purple, just for us. Some of the sky untouched by the sunset was a rich velvety midnight blue and half a moon shone brightly, its reflection danced just before our boat in the water. Our fishing net was protruding to the front of the boat and it looked as though we would catch the moon in our net.

When we first saw Otter Head Island, the sun had just begun to set. The island looked like a giant otter. The Native American perspective was very animated—seeing these land formations as giant creatures. The ideas always seemed to give me pleasure every time I saw one of these things. By the time we reached Otter Head Island it was dark. We could just make out where the lighthouse was and we pulled up to the shore. But it became obvious to us that this was not the normal way to approach the light. I climbed a steep bank up to the lighthouse tower. But there was no way to get in. I told Naomi that there must be another location where there's a dock and a trail to the keeper's quarters. So we shoved off and made our way around the island. I could smell campfire smoke. So someone must be nearby.

We made our way through a channel between two islands. As we rounded a bend, I then saw the light of a campfire. So I figured that's where the dock was. We were both exhausted from our long day's travel. We headed toward the campfire light. To our left, on the other island was a deserted old fish camp inhabited only by a flock of geese. The boat noise and the light from our flashlight disturbed the geese. They all started honking and raising a terrible ruckus. We continued toward the campfire light and could soon see a large dock.

We pulled up closer and could see people. There were quite a few people. But by this time, I didn't care if we were imposing or not. So we pulled up and tied up at the dock. With the geese honking and us pulling up in the dark we probably didn't make a very good entrance. Climbing up on the large concrete dock, I talked with a couple of the men. In the distance we could see the keeper's quarters. There were five or six men there. We soon found out that it was a group of 14 kayakers. They had been dropped off that day from a tugboat that had taken them there from Marathon.

Then when the sun went down it was all translucent moonlight and stars. When we got to Otter Head we found 14 kayakers who had gotten there first. They were nice folks. So we camped near them and they even fed us breakfast. Just as we were getting in bed, a powerboat pulled in too.

The kayakers were going to paddle their way back. The keeper's quarters was already filled with several other people in the party. The option of staying there was out for us. Most of the men weren't overly friendly and the geese were still honking. One older gentleman was friendlier than the rest. He said that he had seen us the day before, going down the Michipicoten River. He said he was surprised to see we had made it this far in only one day. He also said he had owned a Prindle 16 catamaran for many years. He was amazed by our adventure and our idea of traveling around the lake in this type of boat.

The rest of the group seemed a bit reluctant to have us there. But we were too tired to go anywhere else. So we pulled the boat up on shore and set our tent up on the dock. Just as everyone began to settle in, I could hear a powerboat in the distance. It was slowly making its way into the channel. The geese started honking again and a searchlight was sending its beam back and forth. Finally, the boat anchored in the channel for the night. I don't know what time it was when the geese quit honking. But we were in our sleeping bags in the tent and we were falling asleep. What a day!

CHAPTER 18
PLEASURE CRUISE

The next morning, we woke early and started packing. The kayakers were also preparing for their day. They were getting ready to cook breakfast. One of the women was the cook. She invited us to eat with them. We packed our stuff and then had breakfast. We had pancakes, fruit and coffee. It was good. The older gentleman who had owned the catamaran and the lady who did the cooking were only friendly people of the whole bunch. After breakfast, Naomi and I shoved off and waved goodbye.

There was a little bit of activity out on the powerboat that had anchored in the channel. So we stopped by to talk with them. I had hoped to bum a little gasoline for our boat motor seeing it was about 100 miles in any direction to the next place we could buy some more. We pulled up to their boat and I struck up a conversation. The people onboard were from the Minneapolis, Minnesota area. They too had been hoping to stay in the lighthouse keeper's quarters. I assured them that the kayakers would be leaving shortly and they were kind enough to fill our 2½-gallon can with gasoline. We thanked them. We said goodbye and off we went to get some photos of the lighthouse.

It is said that the night the Edmund Fitzgerald sank, the windows in the lighthouse were smashed out by waves and debris, even though they are some 90 feet from lake level. So violent were the waves that night.

We set out from Otter Head early. We were almost out of gas from the day before. So we went and asked the people in the powerboat. They were nice people from Minneapolis, Minnesota. They gave us gas and chatted for a while. It turned out they knew Dad's friend Stephen from Grand Marais, Minnesota. After that, we stopped at a beautiful little waterfall.

Then the wind started coming from the east and we were moving fast.

But today, the sun was bright and the skies were clear. The lake was calm. We could see a waterfall over on the mainland so we took a swing by to get a better look. The waterfall was beautiful. The water cascaded down into two almost identical waterfalls. Naomi and I stopped to take some photos. Then we were back on our way.

The weather couldn't have been better. By mid morning a nice breeze

had picked up, pushing us in exactly the right direction. There is no better feeling on this earth than to be sailing along at a good speed on a beautiful day, taking in some of the most beautiful landscape on the planet. The
hardships and stress of the past days were forgotten. A kind of happiness
would take over our whole beings and we found ourselves laughing.

Our situation was kind of like that of Ernest Shackleton and his men
who had shipwrecked in the Antarctic in 1914. He and his crew survived
on Elephant Island. Shackleton and eight of his men sailed 800 miles in a
small lifeboat to South Georgia Island. But in order to reach a whaling station he, and two of his men, had to hike across a snow-covered mountain
range. After reaching the summit they realized that didn't have the time or
the strength to climb down before nightfall when temperatures would
plummet. So the men took a coil of rope and tied themselves together.
They slid down the steep embankment on their backs. As they gained
momentum sliding down the mountain at incredible speed, they began to
laugh uncontrollably. They had forgotten the danger they were in or past
suffering.

So Naomi and I sailed along. There was a chain of small islands
almost like a reef that protected many areas along the shore. Of all the
areas along Lake Superior we'd seen, this area was the most rugged. To
me, it looked as though the glaciers had not been gone very long. They
had left this area bare and rocky. The lakeshore itself showed signs of terrible storms. We found huge piles of logs and trees washed up 50 or 60
feet out of the water. This reminded us of the incredible storms that can
take place on this lake.

As the day went by, the winds began to increase. We were sailing
along at top speed in and out of the shelter of the rocky islands. By noon
it began to get rough on the big lake. Sometime later, we decided to pull
into a bay, intending to take a break and have some lunch. Pulling the boat
up, we saw some canoes and kayaks on the shore. Farther down the beach,
we saw the kayakers sitting in the shade taking a break too. Naomi and I
talked with a couple of the folks in the canoes. They were curious about
our boat and our adventure. They said they were waiting for the wind and
waves to settle down before they tried to make it around the next point.
They seemed quite amazed with our sailing craft, which was equipped
with snorkeling gear, fishing tackle and musical instruments et cetera.
One of them said, "You've got everything with you."

Naomi and I went for a dip. I used the snorkel and fins in the cold, clear water. After the swim we decided to make lunch. Naomi cooked macaroni on an open fire while I entertained the canoe people by singing and playing the guitar. As I was singing, two of the guy's daughters came over for a listen. It was quite a concert there in the wilderness on the Canadian shore. The wind began to settle down a little. So we all packed our gear and were off toward Marathon, to the west.

We stopped for lunch on a pebbly beach and met some canoeists and played our guitar and sang for them. One guy was so grateful he gave us some of his funky mango bread.

We sailed out of the bay ready for our next adventure. We encountered gusty winds and large waves around the point. But later, the winds subsided a bit. We sailed past our friends in the canoes, prouder than heck of our little sailboat. We were being pushed along by the wind in some of the most rugged and remote area in North America. I told Naomi that most people never even dream of taking a trip like this. And here we were, actually doing it. We counted our blessings as we sailed between the shelter of some rocky islands and the beautiful Lake Superior shore. It seems we were in the right place at the right time.

Naomi and I continued our journey along the Pukaskwa shoreline. By late afternoon we reached Hattie's Cove. There were high rocks at the entrance of the cove. There was also a fair-sized beach. There were a few people enjoying the beach as we pulled up and got our gear off. There was a large campground there. This was also the park headquarters.

We reached Hattie's Cove Campground right outside of Marathon that night and I finally got my hot shower. It was the best shower ever. We camped on the beach there and I called Mommy from the phone booth there. My only other thought about today was that Otter Head Lighthouse was very pretty in the morning sun.

Naomi and I headed for the showers and got cleaned up. It felt good. It had been a while since we felt warm water. Our spirits lifted a bit and we made calls back home to let everyone know we were safe. At the visitors' center we attended a program put on by young park workers who were probably students. The program told about the park. We went back to the boat feeling refreshed. By now it was quite windy. We cooked supper on an open fire. By the time we finished, it was getting dark. So we pitched our tent on the trampoline of the boat. The wind was a bit cold. But inside our little tent, in our sleeping bags, it was warm and dry. Naomi wrote a bit by the light of her candle lantern.

CHAPTER 19

MARATHON AND PORT COLDWELL

It was a cold windy morning as we broke camp. We got ready to sail. The wind and waves were coming almost directly at us. The wind was funneled into the cove. This made it dangerous for us to launch the boat. With some effort, we shoved off and started the motor. The waves were huge as we made our way out of the cove. The motor nearly came out of the water as we were hit by one wave after another. The boat was barely making any forward progress. The motor made a loud moaning sound as it came out of the water after each wave. Slowly, we made our way out of the cove into the open lake. We were able to turn in an angle that allowed the sail to catch the wind. Once it did, we moved ahead more smoothly. But still, it was a wild ride toward Marathon. The town was some 10 miles in the distance.

We left Hattie's Cove early. The water was very rough and it was misty and chilly. So by the time we got to Marathon we were thoroughly drenched and cold. We pulled up on a pebbly beach not far from the town.

By mid morning we were approaching the town. It sat high on a hill. As we neared the shore we could see someone coming down to the shore to meet us. Naomi and I began to pull the boat up. The visitor also helped us. Her name was Kathy Gagnon. She said she had seen us coming in off the lake. It was cold and we were wet. She asked us if we had eaten any breakfast yet. She invited us to her house. Naomi and I readily accepted her invitation.

Just as we pulled in, we saw someone watching from the lookout point above the beach. When we got there, she was standing on the shore. Her name was Kathy and she helped us pull our boat up and right after a few minutes talking, she invited us right over to her house for breakfast and to dry some clothes.

So first we stopped at the grocery store, then went to her house and she made us delicious pancakes, (which I got the recipe for) and dried our clothes. We sang her a couple of our songs.

Her husband came home for lunch so we got to meet him too. He was very nice too. I fell asleep on their couch while Dad and them talked in the kitchen.

On the way, we stopped at a store for a few supplies. We also refilled our gas can. The woman was obviously a saint. She washed our clothes and fed us without hesitation. Naomi and I rested after breakfast. We told Kathy of our adventures and how thankful we were that she had come along. She told us that she was heavy-hearted over the illness of a friend. So Naomi and I sang a couple of songs for her and had a word of prayer to encourage her. After giving us a ride back to the boat, our host watched us as we shoved off into the open lake. She waved goodbye as we sailed west.

We left Marathon around noonish and by that time it was calm and foggy. I mean really foggy—the kind of fog that's so thick that it clings to everything and you can't see the nose on your face. It was very slow and frustrating trying to get anywhere because you never knew what was an island and what was a bay. We were musing that if we hit a big enough island we could just circle it all day without knowing it.

The fog made everything appear eerie. It was like we were floating along on a big white blob that drifted and twisted its fingers around everything and muffled all sounds except for the drip, drip, dripping of the trees. We had to be careful not lose sight of the shore or we could easily get disoriented and end up in the middle of the lake.

There was a large paper mill and a nice-sized harbor west of town. There were a few fishing boats circling at the mouth of the harbor as we sailed past in the fog. The fog grew thicker and thicker until it was difficult to see the shoreline. We groped our way along the shore, trying to make some progress. The difficulty of this method of travel was that when we came to a bay or an island, it was hard to tell if we were following the shoreline or a large island. We could have gone in circles for quite a while and not known it.

We stopped at an island for a while. It had a Pukaskwa pit, a stone cave and midget birch trees. It was cool, so we ghosted silently along the shores until we got to Port Coldwell.

By mid-afternoon we stopped on an island. The fog had lifted a little. We found a spot that looked interesting. There was a large field of stones covering half the island. We expected to find some Pukaskwa pits here and we did. There were some small birch trees that had grown out of these piles of stones that somehow were beautifully shaped by the wind and weather. They were spaced intermittently like someone had placed them there in this beautiful rock garden park.

There was one Pukaskwa pit overlooking the channel between the island and the mainland. No one knows for sure the purpose of these pits. But they were usually located in a place overlooking the lake where the beautiful surroundings turned ones thoughts to the Great Spirit. If they were made for some religious ceremonies, they were surely in good places.

Naomi and I shoved off and made our way along the shore. The fog settled back in again as we made our way past bays and islands. In one bay we found a fishing tug anchored. So we took a few photos. It made an interesting scene for us there in the fog.

Late in the day, as we followed the shore, I could tell that we were out of the wind a bit. Perhaps we were in the shelter of some island. As we made our way along, Naomi and I kept our eyes open for a campsite. Then we saw a large flat rock that might possibly work. But we kept going. After a while we came across what looked like an old shipwreck sticking up out of the water. Upon closer inspection it appeared to be some sort of mining barge. We later learned the barge was used for mining gravel when the Canadian-Pacific Railroad was built along the shore. The barge's steam boiler and machine works were lying there half-submerged in the shallow water. A beaver hut built on top was the only sign of life that had used the barge in the recent past.

There were many wrecked ships along the shore. The most interesting was a huge old barge that loomed up out of the mist like the twisted skeleton of some ancient leviathan. We found a really cool rock to camp upon in Port Coldwell. It was a big rock out in the channel. Wow. I haven't written in a couple of days. A lot has happened since I last wrote. We left Port Coldwell around 8 a.m. and headed for Terrace Bay. I have to start writing in this more I'm starting to forget stuff.

Feeling our way through the fog, we continued along the shore not finding a good camping spot. We came to a large rock cliff. Following the cliff at the water's edge, we felt the temperature drop and the wind pick up a little. I told Naomi that we must be back into the open lake.

"Let's turn around and go back to that flat rock and camp," I said.

"Okay, dad. That looked like the best spot."

We would find the nearest spot to camp and set up the tent for the night. So we backtracked for about a half hour, past the old barge again and finally we made it back to the large flat rock we had seen earlier. We pulled the boat up and began to set up camp. A flat rock doesn't sound like a very comfortable place to pitch a tent. But compared to the cobblestones we had camped on before, this was great.

During the night, a severe thunderstorm rolled through the area. But we stayed warm and dry in our little tent. The only other sound during the night was from the Canadian-Pacific Railroad train that went by in the distance.

In the morning the fog had lifted. Although it was a bit hazy, we could see much better. The rock cliff that was a half-hour's traveling through the fog was now visible and only 75 yards from our campsite. Our perception was much better without the fog.

Naomi and I now decided we must be in Port Coldwell. Years ago, there had been a small town here in 1910. The family of Henry Gerow and his six sons were commercial fishermen here. There was a little store near the Canadian-Pacific Railway Line. But now, the only signs of human activity were the old barge and a couple of old hulks that had once been wooden boats lying along the shore.

Naomi and I broke camp early again and headed west. The winds were still very light, causing us to use our motor a lot and use up our small supply of gasoline. Just about the time we ran out completely, the sun came out and the breeze picked up. The wind filled our sails. Studying our map we figured we could stop at Jackfish Bay and get some gasoline. We pulled up at the mouth of the river. But after looking around we decided we needed to be on the other side.

We headed for Jackfish Cove. It was a bad day for sailing—foggy, no wind and almost out of gas. We prayed and God really blessed. We pulled into Jackfish Bay on our last bit of gas. Just as we approached the bay, the fog lifted, the air brightened and the sun came out. A nice breeze in the sails pushed us into the bay. It was then we discovered from reading

Bonnie Dahl's cruising guide that the town of Jackfish no longer existed.

A strong current kept us from going up the river and with no gas we couldn't use the motor. So we launched the boat into what were now big breakers. We tacked out far enough to reach a point across the mouth of the river. We found a path heading toward some cabins. At one of the cabins we found three guys building an addition. Naomi and I talked with them. They said there was no longer a town at Jackfish Bay. But they did give us enough gasoline to fill our can. They told us about the Slate Islands. There were caribou on the island and also some cabins that the owners left open to whoever wanted to use them.

But there were some cabins there with people working on them—two old people with heavy accents—a middle-aged guy and a big old guy who looked like Santa Claus. They were very nice and gave us some gas. We headed off towards Terrace Bay, bypassing the Slate Islands (which I hear are crawling with caribou). They say there are nice cabins out there open to boaters. I will have to go over there sometime.

Naomi and I thanked them and made our way back to the beach, which stretched for several miles. In the distance were the Slate Islands, looking very beautiful in the midday sun some 10 miles away. Naomi and I would sure like to explore them. But we decided to keep going. We again swore we would make our "Island Tour" another season.

CHAPTER 20

SHIPWRECK

We sailed west under fair skies. The winds were favorable that day until we got close to Terrace Bay. A thunderstorm was quickly moving in with great bolts of lightning and thunder crashing loudly. We headed for the nearest spot to pull in. We got the boat pulled up. It was beginning to rain. So we took the rain fly for the tent and bent down a little tree. We threw the rain fly over it, making a little shelter. Then Naomi and I built a fire to make a hot cup of mocha. We also wanted to use the fire to warm ourselves.

Just before Terrace Bay, a thunderstorm overtook us and we had to pull up on a pebbly beach and throw the rain fly over a tree. We quickly built a little fire and made some hot mocha and passed the time not unpleasantly. Thus the mocha tent was born. It was the first of many. After the storm broke, we set out for Terrace Bay again.

Fortunately, the storm didn't last long. Soon we were on our way again. After sailing a while, we pulled up on a beach near Terrace Bay. We were near the mouth of a river that had a large waterfall.

Naomi and I caught a ride into town with an older couple from Rossport, Ont. The woman said that her son had a large trimaran (meaning three hulls) sailboat at Rossport. She was meeting him there the next day. Naomi and I had a meal at a restaurant and picked up a few supplies. We also found some maps at the visitors' center. One of the boys working there gave us a ride back down to the boat. We thanked him and we were on our way again.

Soon, we pulled up on the beach near a waterfall. It was the biggest Canadian city we had been to yet, about 6,000 people. So they had just about everything we needed. We went out and ate Chinese food. Then we went to a tourist info place to get a map. A young Canadian guy took us back to the beach. We hitched a ride to town with an elderly couple who own a trimaran in Rossport.

By evening we were somewhere near the Schreiber Channel. The islands offered us some protection from the open waters of Lake Superior. As we entered the channel and began to look for a place to camp for the night, the sun was setting. As we were setting up camp, the red and gold of the sunset gave us a spectacular view, making us feel welcome on this rugged Canadian shore.

We sailed for Rossport again that evening, but only made it to a little channel outside of town. We camped on a rock island that had little bluebells growing all over it. It was a very pretty spot.

Our camp was overlooking the place of another interesting shipwreck. But this was no ordinary shipwreck. The 185-foot, 385-ton luxury yacht *Gunilda* was owned by one of the richest men in the world—William Lamont Harnkness. He was the heir of his father-in-law's Standard Oil Company fortune. Harkness and his family were enjoying a leisurely trip along the Canadian shore. It was 1911. Harkness had a professional captain and crew of considerable size. But there is a saying that says, "Pride goeth before destruction." And it certainly was true in this case.

Days before at Coldwell Harbor, Harkness had made it known to locals that he was headed for Rossport and then on into Nipigon Bay. A thoroughly experienced local man named Donald Murray offered to pilot the *Gunilda* into Nipigon Bay. He would do this for the sum of $15. Despite his wealth, Harkness brusquely rejected the offer saying it was too much. The next day, while Harkness was loading coal at Jackfish Bay, similar inquiries brought an offer from Harry Legault to pilot the boat to Rossport. He wanted $25 and train fare back. Although Captain Corkum and his crew thought this was a reasonable offer, Harkness was outraged at the preposterous fee and dismissed the whole idea. Entering Schreiber Channel, the captain saw no shoals marked on their U.S. navigational charts. If they would have had Canadian charts, McGarvey's Shoal would have been marked. But with 300 feet of water showing on his chart, he confidently shoved the engine telegraph to "full ahead."

The *Gunilda* cruising ahead at full speed was a thing of beauty. With the same arrogance surrounding the ocean liner Titanic, which would sink a year later, the *Gunilda* was blindly racing ahead in the pride of wealth and security. Harkness and his family were enjoying the scenery. Suddenly, there was a tremendous shock, which threw the passengers and crew into disarray. The shelves onboard were cleared of the yacht's prized china.

The force of the collision caused the ship to be carried 85 feet up onto McGarvey Shoal. There she sat with her bow breaching out of the water. One of the grandest yachts the world had ever seen was now helpless. The captain and crew were able to take the lifeboats into Rossport where the owner was able to telegraph for a wrecking tug from Fort William, which was over on Thunder Bay.

When the tug *James Whalen* arrived, Harkness was eager to re-float his yacht. But the experienced Capt. Whalen suggested there was a danger of the boat "misbehaving." He suggested that he return to Thunder Bay to retrieve two barges to support the aft end of the yacht.

"Never mind that," Harkness snapped. "Just pull her off."

"But suppose she lists or twists?" Whalen said. "I still think we should have a couple of scows lashed to her."

"Pull! Just pull," Harkness yelled.

The tug captain did just that. After several attempts, the *Gunilda* began to move. But instead of sliding evenly into the water, she took a starboard list. Her aft rail went under, causing her to gulp in large amounts of the cold water of Nipigon Bay. So simple had the salvage operation appeared that no one had closed the portholes or secured the companion way doors. In a few minutes it was all over. The *Gunilda* slid backwards and disappeared into 300 feet of water. And there the mighty yacht rests to this day. What had once been one of the finest ships in the world was now silent in the icy depths of Lake Superior.

The red and gold of the sunset over the wild and lonely wave-lapped shores of Lake Superior made it even more unbelievable that just outside our tent door in the Canadian wilderness lay this once beautiful ship. This was indeed silent testimony to the pride and arrogance of wealth. Naomi and I slept peacefully that night. Our 16-foot sailboat was pulled safely onto shore next to the tent. The lapping of the waves on the shore was the only sound.

CHAPTER 21
ROSSPORT

The morning light came early. Again, we broke camp soon after we woke and we headed for Rossport. The winds were steady, giving us fair progress under sail. By noontime the winds began to fade. Reluctantly, I started the boat motor and we continued on. There were some small islands off to our starboard side.

We woke at the crack of dawn, but it was still too late to escape the thunderstorm, which overtook us at the mouth of the channel. We made a mocha tent, but it was by far the most miserable one. It leaked. It was cold—very smoky. Then I accidentally spilled the mocha on the fire and put it out and we couldn't start it again. So we dozed miserably until the storm abated and we could go on.

The skies were mostly sunny with a light haze in the air. The conditions were a bit better than they had been the last few days. Behind us and to our far left I noticed a fog bank rolling in. I thought nothing of it as we had seen a lot of fog lately. It did look a bit different though. It looked more like a low-lying cloud spreading across the water than fog. Naomi and I continued on. We thought we could see Rossport in the distance, maybe 5 or 6 miles away. We were eager to reach the town and had been thinking about a hot shower and a little rest and relaxation. We were moving steadily along. All of a sudden Naomi looked behind us and yelled: "Look at that cloud!"

We finally got in Rossport Bay. It was calm and we were motoring peacefully along. I saw a strange white cloud out on the horizon. It was very white, very low and was very rounded. I would have to say it was the strangest cloud I'd ever seen.

I glanced over my left shoulder as Naomi grabbed the camera and snapped a pictured. The cloudlike fog bank now looked like a giant tidal wave sweeping down on us with incredible speed. We still had our mainsail up.

I hollered to Naomi, "Get to the back of the boat."

I turned the boat downwind to absorb some of the shock that was about to hit us. We wanted to distribute our weight to the back of the boat to keep the bows from going under. Within seconds, the winds hit us like a bomb going off. The force nearly picked the boat up out of the water. We were catapulted ahead. It seemed as though we were on ice skates as the force of the wind carried us ahead. Suddenly, the mainsail gibed across to the other side with a tremendous crash. The mainsail rope and pulley swung across wildly, catching my right shoulder.

"Watch out, Dad!"

I ducked to keep the boom from hitting my head. The force almost knocked me off into the water.

"This is it," I thought to myself.

But I quickly regained my balance and grabbed the steering tiller. I pointed to a small channel between two islands. The boat raced ahead. If we were to hit those rocks at this speed, we would be smashed to bits. This was no ordinary blow. This was what Stan Rogers, the Canadian songwriter, called a "white squall." And we were in it.

Fortunately, I was able to steer the boat into the channel between the islands, carefully guiding the boat into the lee side of the island where Naomi and I pulled the boat up. Waiting out the storm, we breathed a sigh of relief and had a short prayer of thanks to God for helping us through the storm. There were many times along this trip when the danger was great. But the Lord guided us through.

PSALM 107

Those who go down to the sea in ships
Who do business on great waters
They have seen the works of the Lord
And His wonders in the deep
For He spoke and raised up a stormy wind
Which lifted up the waves of the sea
They rose up to the heavens they went down to the depths
Their soul melted away in their misery
They reeled and staggered like a drunken man
And were at their wits' end

Then they cried to the Lord in their trouble
And He brought them out of their distresses
He caused the storm to be still
So that the waves of the sea were hushed
Then they were glad because they were quiet
So He guided them to their desired heaven
Let them give thanks to the Lord for his lovingkindness
And for His wonders to the sons of men!
Let them extol Him also in the congregation of the people
And praise Him at the seat of the elders.

The storm didn't last long. As quickly as it had come. It was gone again. We were back on our way. Our spirits were lifted as we set a course again for Rossport. When we arrived there we found a rather quiet reception. We pulled up near the marina. It was a beautiful little town situated along a channel, protected by islands. Life here was slow paced. We made our way to some buildings near the dock. One was a fish and chips restaurant. We asked and found that for a small fee we could take showers and wash clothes, which was certainly nice for all the boaters that passed through here.

After taking hot showers and getting clean clothes on, Naomi and I decided to take a stroll through the village. There wasn't much in the way of businesses. But we did find a small restaurant called "Serendipity Gardens." The front yard was covered with beautiful gardens that gave the place a welcomed charm. Naomi was thrilled with the place. The décor and the music made the meal more pleasant.

After we ate dinner we walked through the rest of the town. It was great to be walking around in dry clean clothes after being on the boat for days and days. Naomi and I returned to the dock just in time to see three large trimaran sailboats tying up at the marina. After helping the occupants tie up, we were invited aboard one of the boats. It was an F-27, a very popular design by Ian Farrier, author of the book *20 Knots if by Sea, 55 if by Land*. These trimarans are a very fast and stable boat design. Their wide beam can be folded together for putting a boat on a trailer and heading down the highway.

The owners were a retired couple from Wisconsin. They said they had put in at Marathon and were headed for Duluth, Minn. Naomi and I would meet them later in the town of Grand Marais, Minn. They would have their boat on a trailer. They would tell us they were tired of trying to tack into the wind and big waves. We knew how they felt. They gave up at Grand Portage. But we would continue on.

CHAPTER 22
ANOTHER STORM

After talking to our friends on the trimaran, we saw another interest-ing boat. It was a large tug that offered ferry service to Otter Head Island and surrounding coastal locations. The tug would even go to the Slate Islands, dropping off kayakers and canoeists at various locations that were usually several days' journey from their destinations.

The owners of the boat were a friendly middle-age couple. They invit-ed us aboard and gave us a tour of their boat. After a short visit, Naomi and I said goodbye and made our way back to our catamaran. Wearing dry clean clothes and with a hot meal in our bellies, we stowed our gear and shoved off. We sailed under fair skies into the Nipigon Bay. The waters of the bay were a bit tamer than those out on the big lake. The only sign of human activity in most places in this area was the Canadian-Pacific Railway, with its huge retaining walls weaving a path along the coast.

Out of nowhere, some dangerous looking storm clouds headed our way. It wasn't long and we were beginning to feel the effects of the storm. Terrifying bolts of lightning and loud thunderclaps sent us scurrying toward the shoreline. Quickly pulling the boat up on land we threw our tent rain fly over a small tree and built a small fire. There we sat through the thunder and pouring rain, sipping on a hot cup of mocha. We tried to stay warm by the fire. As the storm passed, the golden rays of the sun looked like fire in the west, producing a beautiful rainbow in the sky.

When we felt it was safe, we jumped back on our boat and were head-ed west again. Our destination that night was to be The Nipigon Bay Resort. One thing Naomi and I learned about while traveling Lake Superior was that everything is always just a little bit farther than it looks on the maps. It seems there was always one more bay to cross and one more point to go around to reach our destination. This was true in finding the resort. By the time we got there, we were wet, cold and exhausted from fighting the storm. Renting the last cabin available, we carried our stuff from the boat and made ourselves comfortable in the small quarters.

After cooking some supper, we got ready for bed. With our clothes hung out to dry, we had a prayer of thanks to God for bringing us safely through the storms that day. With the lights turned low. Naomi wrote in her journal. It wasn't long until we both fell fast asleep.

CHAPTER 23

SHELTERS AND STORMS

It was the 11th day of our trip. We were about half way around Lake Superior. We had covered about 1,000 miles. Naomi and I felt good about our progress. We also felt good about our boat and how well it was working for this kind of trip. There were a few things we would have done differently. We would have allowed more time for the trip so that we could stay longer and enjoy some of the places we had found. But other than that, we felt confident that we could complete our journey.

In the morning, we cooked breakfast in our cabin. It was nice to use a stove. But the dreary walls of an old cabin were no match for stepping out of our tent and cooking breakfast over an open campfire, with the awesome beauty of Lake Superior all around us. One of the resort guests gave us a ride out to the highway. We went to a small store where we could pick up a few supplies, including a new fishing pole and gas. We had lost the fishing pole we had during one of the storms the day before (another sacrifice to the lake spirits).

Returning to the resort, Naomi and I visited with the resort owners. We shared the plans of our journey. We told them of our intention to stay in the shelter of Nipigon Bay. We would sail back out into the lake through the Nipigon Strait. When they heard this, the resort owners urged us to go on the side of St. Ignace Island facing the lake. Otherwise, we would miss some of the most beautiful scenery on Lake Superior. Taking their advice, we changed our plans to include more of the open waters of the big lake and the scenic side of the island.

We loaded our gear and climbed aboard our trusty old boat. One of the resort guests pushed us out into deeper water. We waved goodbye to our hosts as we made our way across Nipigon Bay toward the Moffat Strait, which was a narrow channel between Simpson and St. Ignace Island. The weather was very calm as we crossed the bay. But as we neared the channel, the winds greatly increased. Under full sail we made good headway through the channel. It was a great day to be sailing through such wild and rocky country. But as we entered the open waters of Lake Superior, dark clouds were fast approaching. We could hear a rumble of thunder in the distance.

I told Naomi we better look for a place to pull up and wait out the storm. We saw a place on one of the islands at the mouth of a channel and quickly pulled up, grabbing our tent rain fly. As usual, I looked for a small tree to bend down and set up our temporary shelter.

A powerboat appeared and came in closer to where we were. Seeing our sailboat pulled up on shore and our temporary shelter, they must have thought we were in trouble. I tried my best to signal to them that we were okay. But they kept trying to come in. The waves were rough and the waters were shallow. I feared for the safety of the people on the boat. They were on a cabin cruiser about 26 feet long. If that boat got caught in the shallow water, it would be pounded to pieces. Again, I tried to let them know we were okay and that they should back off.

A middle-aged man appeared on the deck. He was hollering something to me. But over the sound of the storm and waves, his voice was lost. Finally, he disappeared into his boat and made his way into deeper water and was gone. I was relieved that he didn't catch on the rocks because of us. Thunder and lightning crashed and the winds roared. But surprisingly, only a little rain actually hit us. Naomi was down by the boat and I was by the shelter when I spotted a man who appeared near us. It was the man from the boat. He beckoned me to follow him. We had some brief conversation. He told me there were some shelters on the island that Naomi and I could stay in. Sure enough, there were two tents. One shelter was store-bought. The other was a larger structure made from blue plastic tarps.

The man told us his name and that he was from the area. He knew this location well. These tents served as a fish camp. They were left here for whoever wanted to use them. After showing me the camp, we walked over to the man's boat and he offered me a drink. By this time, the storm had past and the weather was clearing up. The man mixed a brandy and Coke for himself. I drank a pop. As we sat on his boat and talked, it seemed to me that he had already had a few drinks too many. He rambled on a bit about a recent divorce and some other problems. But he did tell me about a cabin near Bowman Island at a place called Squaw Bay.

Some Canadian businessman built the cabin. He said that the cabin and sauna were left open for anyone who wanted to use them. As the weather cleared, I said goodbye to our new friend as he pulled away in his boat. Naomi and I headed back to our boat and in a few minutes we were on our way again, enjoying a fresh breeze and the beautiful scenery.

"The resort owners had been right," I told Naomi. "We would have missed some spectacular scenery had we gone the other route."

"That's for sure," she said.

Later that day, we came across a Canadian flag out on a point. We saw a cabin. It looked like a nice spot to land. So we pulled up on the shore to take a break and stretch our legs a little. The cabin owners came out to greet us.

We visited with them for a while. Then the man invited us in to see his cabin. It was rustic and beautiful. We sat down and he offered us a drink. His wife and daughter joined us. He explained that he had been able to purchase the property from some lawyers who had secured the land through an old mining claim. The government owned most of the land along the shore here. These people were fortunate to own such a beautiful spot.

The man also told us that he ran an auto body repair shop in Rossport. The family used the cabin quite a bit during the summer months. Naomi and I asked them about Squaw Bay. He told us that it was 20 miles farther. He also told us how to find it. So off we went into the sunset, hoping to find the harbor before dark.

We did see one or two more cabins along the way. I was in a hurry to reach Squaw Bay. I saw a rocky shoal protruding out from a point of land. Rather than swinging out wide into open waters, I figured our shallow draft boat would have little to worry about. But when we hit bottom on some rocks I felt pretty stupid. I felt worse after some Canadians who had a cabin nearby were going past in their motorboat. They were probably thinking, "Dumb Americans. What are these pilgrims doing way out here anyway?"

We pulled the boat off the rock without too much difficulty. We were soon on our way unharmed, except for our pride. The sun was getting low in the sky now and we were beginning to wonder if we were going to find this place. I told Naomi, "Watch for the Canadian flag on the point. Then we'll know we are there." Then Naomi reminded me of how everything on the lake is farther away than you think it is.

Just before sunset on this perfect summer's evening, we finally saw the flag at the point. We rounded the promontory and saw the beautiful waters of Squaw Bay. As we entered the harbor it curved around like a snail shell. The harbor was one of the most perfectly protected natural harbors I had ever seen. We came gliding in with our sail still up. We must have been a sight to see with our colorful sail and our gear lashed to the wings. There were three boats in the harbor. As we pulled closer we saw a group around a campfire. Two of the boats looked like cabin cruisers and the other looked like an old fish tug.

One of the people in the party signaled to us, showing us where to pull up. We tied the boat and met the others around the campfire. The group introduced themselves and shared something to eat with us. As we ate we told them about our adventure around the lake. We told them we were now more than halfway around. I'm not sure if they were amazed or thought we were a couple of nuts. But after dinner I took out the old backpacker's guitar and played them a few tunes. I told them that I wrote songs about the Great Lakes and that many of the songs were tunes I had written and recorded onto CDs. I told them that my newest CD was called *Legends of the Great Lakes*, while my first recordings were included on a CD called *Ballad of Seul Choix*.

We all sat up into the night as Naomi and I told stories and sang songs. One couple, Murray and Donna Smeltzer, told some interesting stories from the area themselves. As the glow of the campfire burned lower, Murray and Donna told the story of one of the first lighthouses that had been built on Lake Superior, on the Canadian side. That lighthouse had been built nearby on Talbot Island in the spring of 1867.

Thomas Lamphere and his wife were assigned to the duty as lighthouse keepers on the lonely and remote Talbot Island. All went well there that summer. But when fall arrived, winter storms came early making navigation on the big lake impossible. Ice floes prevented any attempt to take the couple off the lonely island. Accepting their fate, they settled in for a long, cold winter with enough supplies that they figured they could survive until spring.

But part way into the winter, Mr. Lamphere took ill. With no doctor and no assistance, he died, leaving his poor wife alone on the isolated island in the middle of the freezing Canadian winter. Mrs. Lamphere was in a terrible state of grief with no one there to comfort or help her. Unable to dig in the rocky frozen ground of the island, the desperate widow buried her husband the best way she could. She laid his body in one of the crevices in the rocks. She covered him with stones and snow. She boldly tried to face the long days and even longer nights alone.

In early spring, some Indian trappers heard her wailing with grief. Her hair had turned completely white and she had lost her mind because of her isolation and misery. Mrs. Lamphere was taken off the island along with the body of her husband. But some people say that on moonlit nights, when the wind is right, some have heard her cries of grief. They have seen her form roving about the island with her long wild white hair streaming in the moonlight.

The campfire now burned to embers. The boaters all made their way to bed. Naomi and I had the cabin ready to sleep in. But we also had fired up the sauna. We wouldn't miss taking a sauna for all the tea in China. So we baked in the sauna and jumped into Lake Superior. We repeated this process as many times as we could. Then we got dried off and ready for bed in our cabin. The moonlight reflected on the waters of the bay as we drifted off to sleep.

I was suddenly awakened during the night by an awful sound. Naomi was terribly sick. She was throwing up in a bucket in the cabin. I jumped out of bed and grabbed a light, trying to help her. But I felt helpless as she was having excruciating stomach pains. I immediately suspected some kind of food poisoning from some spoiled food from one of the boaters. I didn't have a lot but I gave Naomi some peppermint tea and charcoal tablets. Charcoal is supposed to draw poisons from the body.

It was a terrible night. Naomi was up several times heaving her guts out. I did my best to comfort her and I gave her the tea and charcoal mix. I prayed for her that God would protect her and help her. When you're really in trouble it's important to know that God is there to guide and protect. God answered our prayers. In a couple of hours Naomi's condition improved. But morning came way too soon. Naomi slept in late that morning. She was still a little weak, but okay.

The sun shone brightly. Naomi rested while I packed up our gear. By 10 o'clock or so, Naomi felt well enough to travel. Our boater friends were all leaving too. So we said goodbye and we were on our way. As we motored out of the harbor and we rounded the point, Naomi and I were setting the sail in the event that we would catch some wind.

Distracted by the sail raising process, I steered too far starboard and our propeller struck bottom, causing the boat motor to stall. When I restarted the motor, it would no longer propel the boat forward, but would only make noise.

"I think we broke the shear pin," I said to Naomi as I tipped the motor out of the water. The wind was now changing in our sail. So we steered for shore and pulled up where I could work on the motor. Hopefully, the problem was only a shear pin. I took the propeller off. I could see that a broken pin was indeed the problem. Soon we were on our way again. By this time, there was plenty of wind and we moved along quickly under sail power, in and about the islands and along the rugged coastline.

Later that day, we checked our map and saw that a lighthouse should be coming up on Lamb Island. We found it and stopped to explore and have some lunch. It was a beautiful island. It was very rugged and rocky. Along the shoreline, bright orange lichens were growing on the rocks. From between the cracks of the rocks, an assortment of colorful little flowers was growing. At the lighthouse, the keeper's quarters were in good shape. But the lighthouse tower was now gone, replaced by an ugly steel tower with a light on top. Thank goodness there has been such an effort to save these sentinels of the Great Lakes history. All around the lakes there is a new awareness of our maritime heritage and the struggles our forefathers endured along these wild and rugged shores. This aware-ness is spurring our governments and citizen groups into action to save the lighthouses.

From Lamb Island we again sailed westward making good time with fair winds. By evening, Naomi and I were near Shaganash Island. In the distance we could see the white lighthouse tower standing like a lone watchman over this section of the rocky Canadian shoreline. As we drew nearer to the island, we heard the sound of thunder in the distance. I told Naomi to steer the boat while I got a picture or two of the lighthouse. We pulled up close to the lighthouse and walked over to it to investigate. The door was unlocked so we went in. It was dark inside the tower with a musty odor. We climbed the stairs and opened the trap door to the lantern room. It was a beautiful old lighthouse. The beacon had been automated with a solar panel and battery as its power supply. We crawled through another small door and we were out on the catwalk.

The thunderstorm was now much closer and its rumble was more like the sound of 100 freight trains in the distance. I said to Naomi, "We bet-ter get back to the boat and get things secured for the night. This doesn't sound like an ordinary storm. This is a tornado storm."

Hurrying back to the boat, we launched and made a quick circle around the island. It was a low island and didn't have a lot of trees so it really wasn't the best place to be when a storm like this was approaching. Finding what we thought was the safest spot on the island we pulled the boat as high out of the water as we could. We set up the tent.

I told Naomi, "If things really start blowing we can run into the lighthouse."

The thunder continued to rumble and would not stop.

I said, "If the waves get as big as the night the Fitzgerald went down this whole little island could be awash."

There was a foreboding of great danger as I weighted down the tent with large stones. Naomi and I crawled into our sleeping bags and prayed that God would protect us. I had never seen such huge black clouds. The roar of the constant thunder revealed the massive force of this powerful storm. It started to rain. But not long after, the sound of the thunder grew distant. Thank God the storm was moving away now. We fell asleep exhausted from the day's travel.

Later on the trip we learned that the storm hit the Boundary Waters Canoe Area in northern Minnesota and leveled many square miles of trees. The forest in some areas was so tangled that campers had to be taken out by helicopter. If the storm had hit a more populated area it would have been even more devastating.

CHAPTER 24
SILVER ISLET

The next morning, before leaving, we took one last swing by the Shaganash Island Lighthouse to get a few photographs. The lonely lighthouse, with its white painted siding and red trim, was a picture of serenity that morning. It stood alone on this desolate rocky shore since 1910. How many storms had she seen? How many ships had she warned? The lighthouse marks the isolated passage along the North Channel. There was only a foundation where there had once been a keeper's quarters. So now the lighthouse tower stood there alone. The morning sun reflected off the white sides of the lighthouse seemingly saying, "Have a good day."

As we headed out for a new day's adventure we could see the Black Bay Peninsula in the distance. We could see the Paps Mountains, their conical shapes marking the horizon. They gave us a landmark to mark our progress. It wasn't long until the wind began to get quite strong. We were hoping to reach Silver Islet that day, but the way the wind was picking up I had my doubts. We made our way to the tip of the Black Bay Peninsula. There were a few islands to offer some protection from the big lake. But after that, there was quite a stretch of open water to cross as we sailed for Edward Island. The winds were becoming gusty and contrary, often causing us to unwillingly change the direction of our tack. Finally, after a long struggle, we neared Edward Island.

There were two small islands, which were nothing more than large rocky shoals. But they helped block the waves, which were now large white caps. If we could just stay on the right tack! But the wind kept taking us farther out than we wanted to go. The boat wasn't pointing well at all, causing us no small distress. I finally tried to come on the inside of the island. When we did, we found ourselves in the middle of a huge rock pile. Just a couple of feet below the surface the rudders kicked up with a loud banging noise. Immediately, it was difficult to steer. Naomi was acting as a lookout. She tried to guide me through the rocks. I believe the boat did hit bottom a few times. But finally we began to reach deeper water.

Somewhat protected now, we felt a little safer as we neared Edward Island. This was one of those days when it was a fight to make progress.

More than once we were in danger. It would be a struggle to reach the tip of the island. But a there was a protected channel between the island and another small island. The channel was about a mile or so long. It blocked the wind and waves. This gave Naomi and I a chance to catch our breath. While we traveled through the channel, there were several places where larger boats were anchored. They were travelers seeking protection. Others had docked more permanently. There were a few cabins at this location. One place appeared to have a small marina. Perhaps there was some kind of club or resort there.

It was still fairly early, even though Naomi and I had been traveling for several hours. There wasn't much activity as our little boat sailed past several huge sailboats. It wasn't long and we were back out into open waters, although this time we were on a better tack heading for the Sibley Peninsula. To our left we could see Point Porphyry Lighthouse. We were interested in stopping there. But the winds were building. We decided to try to make it to Silver Islet before they got any worse.

We had a long wild ride, but we made it. The huge rock cliffs of the peninsula were an awesome sight from out on the water. The little town was a welcome sight for two ragged sailors, wet and cold. We sailed into the harbor and pulled up on shore. I lay on the warm rocks in the sun for a few moments. Then we changed into dry clothes and were off to explore the town. There was only one small store in the town and they didn't have much. At the dock we ran into Murray and Donna Smeltzer, the Canadian couple that had the fish tug they had converted into a cruising boat. We had met them earlier at Squaw Bay.

The back of the store had a tearoom with a limited menu of tea, soup and rolls. So we all went together and had lunch. Guess what we ordered? That's right. We had tea, soup and rolls. Naomi and I had left before breakfast that day so we were both plenty hungry. I had two bowls of soup and two orders of rolls. We sat overlooking the water, sharing stories of our travels. It was the beginning of a great friendship. We spent the day together exploring the area.

I must say that Silver Islet was one of the most interesting places we visited. Not only was it beautifully unique, the rich history of the area made exploring the location even more fun. The story of Silver Islet begins on the 10th of July 1868 when prospectors searching for copper went ashore to a small island only 80 feet in diameter, about a mile from shore, while having tea. They discovered silver ore.

In 1870, the first boatload of equipment arrived. In the following 14 years, the mine developed into one of the richest silver strikes of its time. More than $3.5 million worth of silver was removed from the tiny island. Against incredible odds of nature, in probably one of the most inhospitable places on earth, this tiny island rock not only became a working mine but also a small town. The town supported a shaft house and steam hoist, several boarding houses, a blacksmith's shop, a reading room, an office and other buildings. These features were added to the area of the tiny island with the help of rock cribbing.

As the four of us strolled along through the little town, we learned more of the history of the area. Particularly helpful in this endeavor was Jack Drynan, a resident that lived in one of the original houses there. He used his home as a small antique shop. We were invited in. Jack was a walking library of the history of Silver Islet. So we spent some time there in his hand-hewn log house.

He told us about the first mining superintendent or "captain," as he was called. He was 40-year-old William Frue who, with a budget of $50,000, was challenged to begin operations on the islet. If during the first year production he were to match the purchase price of the mine and the money invested in starting operations there, Frue would earn a $25,000 bonus in addition to his $5,000 annual salary. That first year, the mine earned a total of nearly $800,000. Mr. Frue was paid his gratuity.

Not only did Frue go above and beyond the stockholders' expectations, he also invented a new fanning process for refining lower grade ore. He also oversaw operations at the store, shipping and town itself. He was an extraordinary man worthy of history's notice.

Jack told us that the end of the town came in 1884. This happened because a sea captain got drunk and allowed his boat to get frozen in. As a result, a much-needed shipment of coal used to fuel the steam pumps did not arrive. The mine flooded, spelling the end of Silver Islet.

The four of us bid Jack goodbye and continued our walking tour of Silver Islet. Many of the old buildings are still in use along the mainland. The hand-hewn log buildings evenly spaced along the shore make one reminisce about the days of the past. The old store still looks the same as it did in the old photographs. But the big lake has reclaimed the mine and all of its buildings. The small islet is just a barren rock much like the way it looked before the white man came to this lonely isle.

As we made our way along the narrow winding road lined with the old miners' homes, it was easy to imagine ourselves back in the time when the mine was alive. One particular place of interest was the old cemetery, which dates back to the 1800s. The old headstones are worn with age. There are trees growing up out of the gravesites. This is where families laid their loved one to rest until the day Jesus returns, as the apostle Paul says in 1 Thessalonians: Chapter 4; verses 16-18.

"For the Lord himself will descend from heaven with a shout with the voice of the archangel and with the trumpet of God; and the dead in Christ shall rise first. Then we who are alive and remain shall be caught up together with them in the clouds to meet the Lord in the air, and thus we shall always be with the lord. Therefore comfort one another with these words."

From the cemetery we walked back to the lakeshore. As we walked along, I noticed that a sailboat in the bay had capsized. The passengers were trying desperately to right it. But in the wind and large waves, they were not having much success. Soon they would be driven onto the rocks.

Murray and I immediately ran for his boat at the dock, which was about a half-mile away. As we ran by my boat I grabbed my wetsuit. I figured I would have to jump into the cold water. Murray had an aluminum fishing boat tied to this fish tug. As quickly as we could, we jumped in. I untied the boat as Murray started the engine. Soon we were racing to the scene. The size of the waves was tremendous. We reached the troubled boat. We could see another powerboat was towing the capsized catamaran through a narrow channel. Unable to right the boat, this was their only option.

We crested wave after wave, approaching the capsized vessel just as it was towed into the mouth of the narrow channel. The waves were of tremendous size. I jumped into the water to assist the two sailors as we entered the channel. We positioned the boat into safer and calmer waters deep within the bay. We worked together to right the vessel.

I was experienced in this process and I could tell some interesting stories about righting a catamaran. I remember one of the first times I ever sailed my Prindle 16. At that time, the boat was owned by one of my neighbors. I was taking my friend Dave, another neighbor, on a test run across Munising Bay on Lake Superior. I had just assembled the boat a day or so earlier.

Dave had never been on a sailboat. He was amazed at our speed as we zipped across the bay at about 20 knots. Suddenly, we were hit by a heavy puff of wind. We began to ride on one hull. Instinctively, I pulled to release the main sheet to let the wind out of the sail. That's when I discovered the adjustment angle would not let the rope loose. Frantically, I tugged and jerked as we slowly tipped into the cold waters of Munising Bay. The sailboat was half-submerged. I was still unfamiliar with the boat. But I found a line I thought would work as a righting line. Dave and I grabbed hold and pulled with all of our weight. The boat gradually started to come over. The catamaran toppled over and sat upright. I hollered for Dave to climb aboard. We headed back across the bay. When we got to the other shore, I adjusted the angle of the main cleat. That adjustment solved the whole problem. I later bought the boat from my neighbor. I haven't tipped it since that trip with Dave, although I've been close many times.

So I helped the two sailors right their boat. The men were very appreciative. They were cold and were likely experiencing some symptoms of hypothermia. Slowly, the mast rose as their boat righted. It set squarely down on the water and into the wind. The men dropped the mainsail. We were able to find a safe place to keep their boat until the weather settled down. If this narrow harbor had not been almost directly downwind of the sailors, this incident would most likely have had a very different ending.

The men thanked us as Murray and I climbed back into our fishing boat. We headed back out into the lake. We went through the channel entrance and into some very big waves. Fortunately, they were somewhat rolling waves. We received some protection against the open sea from Burnt Island and the landing. Otherwise, I don't think we would have made it ourselves.

We rode through the waves back to Murray's fish tug. There, Naomi and Donna gave us a welcome fit for heroes as we tied the boat up and told them about our adventure. At some point during the day, I had realized it was my birthday. So Murray and Donna invited Naomi and I to supper onboard their boat. We gladly accepted. Our hosts were soon serving us a hot meal in their comfortable galley aboard their tug.

It was a delightful evening. We all shared tales of the lake. The evening wind calmed to a soft summer breeze. This was one of the finest times of our entire trip. We didn't have any birthday cake. So instead, we had sweet rolls I had purchased earlier at the old store tearoom. Donna made a makeshift candle and we all laughed as I blew it out. I was 44 years old and living a dream. I'm happy that these people could share it with me. After supper, Naomi and I sang some of our Great Lakes songs for our hosts. The sun sank low.

Jack Drynan's daughter Tracy came down to the dock. She offered Naomi and I a place to pitch our tent in the their backyard. The yard was just up the hill from where we had pulled up the boat. Tracy's offer was a good thing because there was no good place to camp on the shoreline. It was all large rocks. We said goodnight to Murray and Donna, grabbed our gear and off we went.

In no time, we had the tent set up and we were ready to entertain again. We all sat together on Jack's front porch that overlooked the lake. An older gentleman joined us. He brought his dog along. Everyone drank a few toddies while Naomi and I sang and told stories until our eyelids grew heavy. Then we made our way back to the tent. The warm night air was pleasant as we crawled into our sleeping bags. It was the end of another perfect day.

CHAPTER 25

THUNDER BAY

"Naomi, time to get up," I called. "It's daylight in the swamp."

The dawn had come early. We packed our tent and headed for the boat and the harbor. The tiny village lay silent in the early morning dew. The lake had calmed during the night. That would allow us to make some progress.

I planned on stopping in Thunder Bay to see if I could find some new rubber seals for our dry suits. The lake was still rolling from the day before as we pushed away from the shore. Our Canadian friends were still asleep in their cozy little fish tug. We started our motor and set out for Thunder Bay. The rocky cliffs of Thunder Cape reflected the red and gold of the morning sun. The light gave the cliff faces an almost magical appearance. The weather was perfect. But we felt like a cork on the ocean. In our little boat, we rose up and down on the rolling waves.

Passing Thunder Cape, I said to Naomi, "There's a lighthouse. That's Trowbridge Island Lighthouse."

"Shall we go in and see it?" she asked.

"I don't think so. We have to keep moving if the wind is going to be like it was yesterday. We don't want to get caught out in the open with those kind of waves."

So we passed the lighthouse while a freighter passed us, heading to Thunder Bay. The lighthouse sure did look inviting there in the morning sun. The beacon was built in 1910 to mark the east entrance into Thunder Bay.

Back in 1906, four years before the lighthouse was built, a horrible accident occurred in the area involving the 255-foot, 1,175-ton steamer *Theano* of the Algoma Central Line. The ship tried to reach shelter in 50 mph gusts and pelting snow. She was pushed off course into Trowbridge Island. The boat then swung broadside to the rocky shore, crushing in her side. The 20-man crew remained onboard for two hours. The men worked desperately to try to save the ship. But with water pouring in faster than the pumps could handle, the sailors wisely launched two lifeboats and pulled away.

Moments later, the icy waters touched the red-hot boilers of the boat and the *Theano* blew up. The ship slid off the rock ledge into the depths.

The passing steamer *Iroquois* soon picked up one of the lifeboats. But the second had to fight its way for 20 miles to Port Arthur. Ten men were exposed to the bitter cold for nearly half a day. Had the lighthouse been there, help would have been much closer at hand.

"How are you doing, Naomi?"

"I'm doing okay now that the sun is getting a little higher. I was a bit chilled earlier, but now I'm fine."

She smiled.

"Look, here comes the *Irish Mist,*" I said.

Our Canadian fish tug friends were also getting an early start. It was nearly an hour before they caught up to us and passed us. Murray and Donna sat at their steering station on top of the boat. The happy couple led the way to Thunder Bay. Naomi and I followed as close as we could. But by the time we could see Thunder Bay, the fish tug was just out of sight.

"The breeze is picking up, Naomi. Let's hoist the mainsail."

We jumped into action and we were soon under full sail.

The closer we got to Thunder Bay, the stronger the winds became. They pushed us quickly into the harbor.

"Where shall we land, Pop?"

"Let's pull up over there by the gas dock. We need to get some gas anyway."

There was a grassy spot nearby, so we pulled up and started to unload.

"I'm going to take a shower," Naomi said.

"Okay. I'll get the gas cans filled while you shower."

We went off on our missions. We planned to meet back at the boat and then head into town. Thunder Bay was the first large city we had come to on our trip. We felt a bit out of our element here in the big city.

I filled the gas cans and then waited for Naomi. In a little while, she came back.

"Feel better?" I asked.

"Much better."

She smiled again.

"Are we going to a restaurant?" she asked.

"Yes. Then I'll try to find some new seals for our dry suits."

We found an old train depot that now housed shops and a restaurant. The weather was warm. We sat on the porch and ate lunch. The old building was well suited for its new use. It was close to the harbor and it had that "historic" look.

After lunch, we searched for a place that sold rubber seals. I found a place that had a couple left. But they didn't have everything I needed. They also weren't able to install the seals. We headed back to the boat and got ready to leave. While we were working, an older couple from one of the larger sailboats stopped and asked us about our trip.

"How far are you going?" they asked.

"All the way around the lake."

"What a wonderful trip. I bet you can make some good time on that catamaran," the gentleman said. Then they wished us good luck and watched us sail out of the marina.

Naomi and I were glad to be leaving the big city. The greater distance we were from it, the more we felt at home among the rocky lakeshore, the wind and the waves.

"Look over there, Naomi. There's the Sleeping Giant."

"I can sure see it now, to the east."

The mountains of the Sibley Peninsula form a range whose profile looks like an Indian lying on his back, sleeping. The local Native Americans believed that these rock formations were their ancestors. The Indians thought that if they talked favorably about their predecessors, good luck would come to them.

We sailed quickly past Old Fort William. But the winds became strong and gusty. The waves got larger and larger. We headed for Pie Island. Even though it didn't look like a good spot to land, we sailed there.

"Our goal is to reach Thompson Island before nightfall," I told Naomi. "I heard one of the store keepers say that there's a cabin and a sauna there."

"Sauna?"

"Yes, wouldn't that feel good after fighting the wind and waves?"

We finally made it to Pie Island. With some difficulty, we landed the boat through the waves and rocks. Naomi and I took a break. We considered staying there for the night. But the shore along the lee side of the island offered us no protection from the wind and only a very rocky beach. So after looking around, I asked Naomi if she thought we should try to reach Thompson Island.

She said, "Yes."

I agreed.

We went back into the white caps of Lake Superior and moved west around Pie Island. It seemed the farther we sailed, the rougher the seas got. Suddenly, there was a noise in the distance.

"Oh! Oh," I said. "Did you hear that? Thunder."

"Yes, it's coming our way."

"There's Thompson Island. But there sure is a big stretch of open water in front of us."

"Yeah, I know."

"Those are some mighty big white heads. I think we should find a place to camp back on Pie Island."

Naomi agreed.

We started looking for a place to land, but couldn't find one. All along the northwest shore, the wave-driven rocky coast offered us no good place to land. There was certainly no good place for camping either. After we searched for a couple of miles, the thunder had moved very close. We kept looking for a place to beach the boat.

"It looks like a little stretch of beach up ahead," I said. "Do you see it there?"

"Yes, it looks like an old dock there, or what's left of one."

"Not much protection from the wind. But with that storm coming, we don't have any choice."

By now, the thunder was nearly on top of us. The breakers were huge as we sailed through them up onto the beach. Naomi and I both knew what we had to do. We jumped off the catamaran and pulled the boat out of the water.

"Pull," I yelled. "Pull! Pull! Pull!"

Using our combined strength, we finally succeeded. The thunder hurried us along.

"So much for the sauna tonight," I said, looking out over the angry white waves. "Let's get that tent set up before it pours."

The thunder and the waves were crashing loudly.

We were well trained by now. In an instant, we had the tent set up.

"This looks like some old homestead," I said, glancing around.

We unpacked our gear and climbed into the tent, just as the drizzle turned into a downpour. The thunder and the sound of the rain on the tent were very loud. Naomi lit a candle lantern and wrote in her journal. I read a bit. We said a prayer of thanks for our safe travel. Soon we were fast asleep. It was surprising how comfortable a good tent could be.

CHAPTER 26
GRAND PORTAGE

I woke up early, as usual. I climbed out of the tent and looked around. The sky was overcast. But there was no rain. The lake had calmed down. All the whiteheads were gone. I walked around the clearing. The area was overgrown with saplings. It did appear to be an old homestead. But I didn't find any foundations. "I'd like to know the history of this spot," I thought. "Perhaps it was an old logging or mining camp."

"Naomi, wake up."

I heard some movement inside of the tent. While Naomi was waking up, I began getting ready for another day's voyage. We studied our map and decided that we would try to reach Grand Portage where we could stay in a hotel. That would be a nice change of pace with the way the weather had been acting. We hurriedly broke camp and got the boat ready to shove off.

"We don't want to be caught in this big stretch of open water," I said, as we launched the boat through 1- to 2-foot waves. The winds had dictated where we stayed. We sailed toward the mainland, which I guessed was about ten miles away.

"Now we know why the commercial fishermen get up so early, hey Naomi? So they can get back in before the winds pick up."

Sure enough, we ate breakfast on the boat, while the winds gradually started to build. By noon, the waves were bouncing us around quite a bit. There was some protection from Victoria and McKellar islands. But as we passed them, we would encounter an open stretch of water before we could reach Pine Point.

In the distance, we could see Isle Royale, the largest island in Lake Superior. Naomi and I both longed to see it, with its beautiful bays and rugged coastline. But we couldn't do it now. We had to continue our trek around this giant lake or we might never make it. We both swore that someday we would return for an island tour. We decided we could leave from Minnesota, explore Isle Royale, the Canadian shore, visit the Slate Islands and see Michipicoten Island.

"Maybe even Caribou Island," I said.

"Yeah. What an adventure it will be, Pop."

We both agreed it would be an excellent trip. But for now, the wind and waves were building against us. Once we rounded Pine Point, it was on toward Grand Portage. As we approached Pigeon Point, we let out a cheer because we knew that we were back in U.S. waters. Not that we didn't like the Canadian side. Actually, we loved it. But we were making progress on our voyage and that was the reason for our cheer.

As we passed Pigeon Point, we were exposed to the full fury of the wind and waves. Taking on the ice-cold spray and waves made travel rather miserable. In the distance we could see the Susie Islands.

"We'll get some protection from those islands pretty soon," I yelled, above the wind.

Naomi only nodded. She held on for dear life.

It was only a day earlier, back in 1885, that a ship was lost in this very same spot. The 91-ton *Isle Royale* began to leak in heavy seas near the Susie Islands. The small steamer had served the logging camps and mines of Isle Royale. The boat carried passengers and freight. But now, she was in trouble. The waves pounded the little ship. The seams of the vessel opened. The water rushed in and she began to sink. The passengers and crew were able to launch the lifeboats. They made it safely to the Susie Islands.

Like the crew of the *Isle Royale,* we too were now battling heavy seas. We finally reached the shelter of the islands. There was a large sailboat anchored in the lee of one of the islands. The boat's occupants were probably tired of beating against the wind, like we were. All too soon, we had past the islands. We were back into the strong waves. We hadn't gone much farther when we decided we'd had enough. We started looking for a place to land and wait out the wind.

"If I was smart, I would have pulled in at the island," I said. "Now we don't have a good place to pull in."

"Oh well. Find a place, Dad," Naomi encouraged.

We did find a landing spot, but it wasn't a very good one. It was rather rocky and not too sheltered from the wind. But we made the best of it. We built a fire and cooked some lunch. I tried fishing a bit. After we ate, Naomi picked blueberries. But after awhile we grew restless to get going. I couldn't tell if the wind had died down or not.

"Get ready," I said. "We're going to get moving, waves or no waves."

Again, we headed for Grand Portage. The Ojibwe had called the place *Kitchi-Onogaming*, "the great carrying place." The name was later changed to Grand Portage by the French. Grand Portage became a major gateway into the interior of North America for exploration, trade and commerce between Lake Superior and Montreal, with westward systems of lakes, rivers and interior trading posts, which eventually reached the Arctic, the Bevort Sea, and the Pacific Ocean.

During the late 18th Century, Grand Portage served as the inland headquarters for the Northwest Fur Company and was the location for a summer rendezvous involving Indian families, French voyagers, Scottish Clearks, Pays Den Haut wintering partners and Montreal and London agents.

My great-grand parents on my father's side were French Canadian (Indian?). Perhaps, somewhere in the distant past, my ancestors had traveled these waters before us. Was this the voyager spirit being relived through my adventure with Naomi?

We had our hearts set on that warm shower and bed that we knew would be waiting. After being cold and wet all day, we would get to that hotel, come hell or high water. The weather calmed a bit. By dusk, we pulled into Grand Portage. We both got a hot shower and afterwards, we ate a good meal in the restaurant. We were in much better spirits. We even sang a couple of Karaoke tunes in the lounge. It was our own kind of rendezvous.

"Well, we're in the home stretch," I told Naomi.

We felt proud of our progress. That evening, I called ahead to Grand Marais, Minnesota, which was the next town on our itinerary. I left a message for Steve Hoglund. He was an old high school chum of mine. I told him we would be in Grand Marais the next day.

We had learned that one of the keys to successful sailing was that early morning travel before the lake got rough. So again, very early, Naomi and I set out to get as far as we could before the waves got to building. Sure enough, by 10 o'clock or so, we were heading right into the heavy wind and waves.

Again, we found a spot to land. We pulled the boat up onto shore. We were right near Highway 61, which runs along the north shore in Minnesota. So we decided to hitchhike to the nearest store and get some more gas and a few supplies.

It wasn't long before we got a ride with a couple of young people in a pickup truck. Like us, they were traveling around the lake. They gave us a ride to the next town, Hovland. The town consisted of basically just a store with a gas pump. But that's all we needed.

We talked with the couple, as we were getting our supplies, and we discovered that our hosts were brother and sister. We also found out that they had a guitar. We started playing it in the parking lot of the store. We were soon having a great time playing and singing songs. They said they weren't in a big hurry and they could bring us back to our boat. Naomi and I thanked them and we invited them to have lunch with us.

Back at the catamaran, we built a campfire and ate lunch. Then we showed them our boat and how we survived in the wild. We all had a great time. But as we finished lunch I noticed something.

"Hey, the wind changed," I said.

The shifting air had changed to an offshore breeze.

So quickly, we said goodbye to our friends and set out for Grand Marais. The offshore breeze pushed us along on a broad reach, the fastest tack for our boat. Believe me, when a catamaran is on a broad reach with an offshore wind, you're really moving.

"Yippee," we hollered

Each puff of wind pushed us nearer to our destination. But the offshore winds began building. And soon, what had been gentle breezes became stronger and stronger gusts of wind. Then, all of a sudden, we were hit again. The boat was pushed up on one pontoon. I fumbled to release the main sail. But with the force we were struck with, I thought we were going to capsize.

When I released the main sheet, the boat hung there for a moment, suspended in midair. Naomi and I were holding on as tight as we could. We knew that we probably would not last long if we fell into that ice-cold water. But then, like some old dog, the catamaran shook herself and turned upright again. The starboard side pontoon came slapping down into the water. The boat lunged ahead. Another gust hit hard and nearly capsized us again.

"Let's pull into shore and reef the main sail," I yelled.

Naomi agreed. She was still half in shock, still holding on tight. After reefing the main sail and taking in the jib, we got back underway. Wouldn't you know it? The wind had changed and so we went back to bucking the waves again. Finally, we made it into Grand Marais Harbor just before sunset.

"Let's pull up right in front of the hotel," I said.

We beached the boat, grabbed our gear and booked a room. I went to look for my old high school friend while Naomi got ready for dinner. There was no one around when I found his place. I left a note and went back to the hotel. While Naomi and I were having dinner, Steve showed up.

"I didn't think you would make it here today with the winds the way they were," he said, sitting down next to us.

"It was only by sheer determination," I said.

I told him about our travels that day. It was good to be in Grand Marais. We toasted our successful arrival. Grand Marais is a popular tourist spot for travelers going north along Lake Superior or camping in the Boundary Waters Canoe Area.

We thought the town was a delightful place to visit. So we stayed an extra day for a little rest and relaxation. In the evenings we sang our ballads about the lakes, sea captains and shipwrecks. Our audiences were quite amused, especially when we sang about the notorious Captain Bundy and his gospel ship, sailing into Grand Marais to save the sinners.

"That song is my Great Lakes version of Neil Diamond's 'Brother Loves Traveling Salvation Show,'" I said.

But Captain Bundy was a real person. They say he was quite a wild character in his day, a lot of drinking and fighting. He went to a revival meeting to scoff the preacher and cause trouble. Instead, he ended up getting converted and spent the rest of his life as a gospel preacher, a kind of circuit rider on the Great Lakes.

They say he had a deep thundering voice that could be heard over a mile. He'd start preaching before he got to shore and he'd ring the ship's bell. Then he'd set up his tent and have a revival service.

Captain Bundy's Gospel Ship
By Carl Behrend

Captain Bundy's Gospel Ship
Is sailing in the bay
I hear that bell ringing
I hear that organ play
I hear the captain shouting
O'er the crashing of the waves
We've got to save some sinners
Before we sail away

Sail away, sail away
We've got to save some sinners
Before we sail away

The captain was a sailing man
Of many stormy seas
Drink and swear and cuss and fight
He'd do just what he pleased
They say he was a scoffer
Just as proud as he could be
The revival that he went to scoff
He wound up on his knees

Sail away, sail away
We've got to save some sinners
Before we sail away

The Gospel Ship is leaving port
The tent's all packed away
The captain's words have all bee preached
His prayers have all been prayed
Superior shores are calling me
I heard the captain say
We've got to save some sinner
Up there in Grand Marais

Sail away, sail away
We've got to save some sinners
Before we sail away

All too soon, the evening ended.

The following morning, it was back on the boat again at daybreak. Clearing the Grand Marais break wall, we waved good-bye to our friends we had met there and we sailed off through the rolling waves.

CHAPTER 27
TWO HARBORS

It was a typical morning as we sailed westward. As usual, the winds came up about 10 o'clock and we had to pull into shore and wait it out again. By this time, Naomi and I were both tired of fighting the wind, waves and ice-cold Minnesota water. The current churned the surface waters cold. This made the air temperatures cold there, even on a 90-degree day. We were soaking wet and cold all day long.

I told Naomi, "Tonight, when the winds die down, we are going to motor this boat all night and we're going to get out of Minnesota and this damn north shore wind."

Naomi agreed.

That evening, when the winds began to drop, we motored into the night. We took turns steering the boat. It was a cold night out on the lake. But as we traveled, the moon came out and the stars were clear and bright. We had no running lights. But we kept a flashlight handy. Our 3-horsepower motor pushed us along at about 5 1/2 miles per hour on the GPS.

Even though it was cold, it was a beautiful night on the lake. To top things off, the northern lights came out to guide us on our way. With their constantly changing beauty, the aurora borealis was a wonder to see. We felt like the children of Israel being guided by the "pillar of fire" by night.

We took turns at the helm throughout the night. We also took turns sleeping. We had laid a sleeping bag on deck. We covered up with the main sail to try to block the wind. By morning, the splashing waves had gotten the sleeping bag wet. By dawn, we were both froze. But we kept going.

We took some pictures as we passed the Split Rock Lighthouse. It was a beautiful morning. The lake was now quite calm. A cold mist was rising up out of the water, which was met by the rays of the early morning sun. The huge rocky cliffs of Split Rock were reflected on the water painting us a picture we will never forget.

We kept going until we neared Castle Danger, where we found a place to pull up. Both of us were shivering. We built a campfire and cooked breakfast. We spent some time just trying to warm up. After awhile, a man who owned the beach we had landed on approached us. He was friendly.

We were able to bum some boat gas from him. He pointed out Bark Point, Wisconsin on the other side of the lake. He said it was about 25 miles away.

After thanking him for the gas, we were on our way again. We kept going until we reached a place called Lafayette Bluff. The bluff is near Encampment Island, about five miles northeast of Two Harbors. I told Naomi we were going to cut across the lake.

"I'm tired of fighting this wind," I said.

"If you think so, Pop."

So at Lafayette Bluff, we headed for the Wisconsin shore. They say the bluff was named after a famous shipwreck, which happened nearby. The 454-foot steel steamer *Lafayette* and her 436-foot barge *Manilla* were caught out on the lake in a terrible northeast storm. Blown off course and blinded by snow, both ships were blown up onto the rocks near the bluff. The *Lafayette* broke in half in three minutes. Some of the crew from the barge was able to climb ashore. They threw lines to sailors on the stern section of the *Lafayette*. Crewmen used the ropes to escape the doomed vessel. While crossing to safety, a fireman named Patrick Wade slipped from the rope to his death. The rest of the crew made it safety.

Those men on the bow section of the ship, including Captain Wright, were able to jump to the rocks. They then climbed the rocky cliff. The survivors suffered miserably that night in the blowing gale. They built a makeshift shelter and fires. But many suffered from frostbite and exposure.

The next day, the storm had subsided. The beleaguered crewmen made their way back to shoreline. The *Manila* was still fairly intact. The men were able to find food and shelter there where they were rescued a couple of days later. The name Lafayette Bluff has remained to this day.

Sailing out across the lake, we headed for the Wisconsin shore.

"We're getting out of Minnesota," I told Naomi.

"Whatever you think, Pop."

Tired of fighting the wind and the waves, we left Lafayette Bluff behind us growing smaller in the distance. We knew it was pretty risky business to cross 25 miles of open water. But we were desperate from fighting the weather and cold water.

"When we get to the Wisconsin side, the winds should be behind us," I said.

"That will be nicer sailing."

Naomi grew rather quiet at the prospect of crossing the open lake in our little boat.

"We'll probably save three days' time by crossing here," I said. "We have to be back by August 8th for grandma and grandpa's 50th wedding anniversary."

Naomi agreed. But she was still rather quiet.

We had only the jib sail up because the winds had been rather strong the past few days. We didn't want to be overpowered and capsize way out in the middle of the lake.

"We should be able to handle some pretty rough weather," I said confidently, as the waves grew larger. Though we had set our course for Bark Point, the wind and waves wanted to push us more to the east. The waters of Lake Superior can look mighty big when you're out there in a small boat. It reminded me of a story I once read of in annals of the early shipping days on the Great Lakes.

An Indian had been a passenger aboard a ship that hit some high seas.

"There's some mighty tall water here," he said as he watched the waves.

Now the water was tall for us. And it was getting taller.

"I don't think we're in any danger," I said.

I made the statement confidently, but I was beginning to doubt the wisdom of crossing here.

Naomi didn't answer.

I think she was praying.

We were both rather quiet for a while.

During our voyage around the lake, Naomi would often recite poems. One poem she quoted sections of quite often Henry Wadsworth Longfellow's *The Wreck of the Hesperus*. The poem is about an over confident sea captain sailing into a winter gale with his young daughter onboard. Both are killed.

I would often ask Naomi to quote the poem as we sailed. But now, the words took on a more serious meaning while the waters around us grew taller. I certainly wasn't asking her to quote from it now.

No matter how bad things seemed, we couldn't turn back now. The wind and waves would never let us return the way we came. We must go with them and continue across. Silently, the words of the poem raced through my head. Was I now the foolish captain?

It was the schooner Hesperus, *that sailed the wintry sea;*
And the skipper had taken his little daughter to bear him company.
Blue were her eyes as the fairy-flax, her cheeks like the dawn of day,
and her bosom white as the hawthorn buds that ope in the month of May.
The skipper he stood beside the helm, his pipe was in his mouth. And
he watched how the veering flaw did blow the smoke now west, now south.
Then up and spake an old sailor, had sailed to the Spanish main,
"I pray thee, put into yonder port, for I fear a hurricane."
"Last night, the moon had a golden ring. And tonight no moon we
see!"
The skipper, he blew a whiff from his pipe, and a scornful laugh
laughed he.
Colder and louder blew the wind. A gale from the Northeast, the
snow fell hissing in the brine and the billows frothed like yeast.
Down came the storm, and smote amain the vessel in its strength;
She shuddered and paused, like a frighted steed, then leaped her cable's
length.
"Come hither! Come hither! My little daughter, and do not tremble
so; for I can weather the roughest gale that ever wind did blow.
He wrapped her warm in his seaman's coat against the stinging
blast; he cut a rope from a broken spar, and bound her to the mast.
"Oh father! I hear the church bells ring, Oh say, what may it be?"
"'T is a fog bell on a rock-bound coast!" And he steered for open
sea.
"O father! I hear the sound of guns, oh say, what can it be?"
"Some ship in distress, that cannot live in such an angry sea!"
"Oh father! I see a gleaming light, oh say, what may it be?"
But the father answered never a word, a frozen corpse was he.
Lashed to the helm, all stiff and stark, with his face turned to the
skies, the lantern gleamed through the gleaming snow on his fixed and
glassy eyes.
Then the maiden clasped her hands and prated that saved she might
be; and she thought of Christ, who stilled the wave, on the Lake of Galilee.
And fast through the midnight dark and drear, through the whistling
sleet and snow, like a sheeted ghost, the vessel swept towards the reef of
Norman's Woe.
And ever the fitful gusts between a sound came from the land; it was
the sound of the trampling surf on the rocks and the hard sea sand.

The breakers were right beneath her bows, she drifted a dreary wreck, and a whooping billow swept the crew like icicles from her deck.

She struck where the white and fleecy waves looked soft as carded wool, but the cruel rocks, they gored her side like the horns of an angry bull.

Her rattling shrouds, all sheathed in ice, with the masts went by the board; like a vessel of glass, she stove and sank, Ho! Ho! The breakers roared!

At daybreak, on the bleak sea-beach, a fisherman stood aghast to see the form of a maiden fair, lashed close to a drifting mast. The salt sea was frozen on her breast, the salt tears in her eyes; and he saw her hair, like the brown seaweed, on the billows fall and rise.

Such was the wreck of the Hesperus, in the midnight and the snow! Christ save us all from a death like this, on the reef of Norman's Woe.

As we approached the shipping lanes, a freighter appeared in the distance. It appeared to be heading in our direction. Would our paths meet? Remembering our last close encounter with a freighter, I knew it was possible to get in their way. I held the boat on a steady course. I would not allow us to fall into a trough and possibly broach in the waves.

Warily, we kept an eye on the freighter looming ever larger in our path. I knew we didn't want to be in its path. Fortunately, the freighter passed us about a mile away. That was fine with us. With that danger behind us, a new danger appeared. The waves seemed to be getting bigger. The wind was shifting around, making it difficult to hold a steady course.

"Dammit," I muttered.

It's a good thing Naomi was praying because the wind clocking like that really gets me angry. After what seemed like an eternity, the distant shore grew closer. The nearer it came, the more our tensions eased. We finally began to be able to make out the cliffs and hills on the distant shoreline. Our anxiety turned to joy. Our talk became more cheery now. I think I even asked Naomi to quote some of the "Hesperus."

We approached the Bayfield Peninsula.

"Look, I see one of the Apostle Islands," I said.

"Oh yeah. I see it."

We then we made another discovery that made our spirits soar even higher.

"Feel the water," I said.

Naomi dipped her hand in the water. Her face grew brighter.

"It's warm," she said, in disbelief.

"The winds must blow the warmer surface water over to this side of the lake," I said.

I don't think that you could have found two happier sailors in the whole world, as we were that evening. We made it to Squaw Bay and we pulled the boat up on a beautifully forested sandy beach. I leapt from the boat and joyfully kissed the ground. Our hearts light, we secured the boat and began to set up camp. The high winds had now softened and turned to a relaxing breeze. We sat by our campfire overlooking Eagle Island. Together we watched a beautiful sunset over the most beautiful lake in the world.

CHAPTER 28
THE APOSTLE ISLANDS

The next morning, we woke up in our cozy little tent and warm sleeping bags to the welcome sound of waves lapping against the shore. We raced through our morning chores. There was a sense of peace, mixed with adventure: peace, knowing that the prevailing winds would now be behind us; adventure and excitement, knowing that we would be sailing through the Apostle Islands and on to Bayfield.

We soon launched the boat and bid goodbye to our campsite. We could see some commercial fishermen in the distance checking their nets.

"Should we get some fresh fish?" Naomi asked.

We decided not to because we would probably be stopping in Bayfield later that day and eating dinner in a restaurant. But it was nice to have that option available. We sailed under a reefed mainsail in a fairly good wind, which was going our way. When we sailed past Sand Island and around the northern tip of York Island, we came into the lee of York Island. It soon became obvious that we were overdressed and under-sailed for this southern side of the lake. We pulled into a bay on the island and took off our foul weather gear and pulled the reef out of the mainsail.

The sun shone warmer now and, with the warmer water currents, we felt like we were in the Caribbean Islands instead of on Lake Superior. Our sense of happiness was indescribable.

"I wish we could explore all of these islands," I said.

"We'll have to come back next year," Naomi said. "On our island tour."

We both laughed.

A nice breeze scooted us along. We passed Raspberry Island and we took a few photos of the lighthouse as we passed.

The following summer, I did return and I visited all of the lighthouses of the Apostle Islands. Unfortunately, Naomi had other plans. She couldn't make it. While visiting the Outer Island Lighthouse on that trip, I had lunch with a volunteer lighthouse keeper. Afterwards, I played him a couple of my songs about the Great Lakes, including "Captain Bundy's Gospel Ship."

"Captain Bundy?" he exclaimed. "I think he stayed here."

He looked through a lighthouse keeper's log. Sure enough, there it was. In an entry dated August 20, 1879 was written: "Glad Tidings gospel ship arrives with Captain Bundy. Preaches a sermon, a.m. Leaves for Willis Island, p.m."

Even though Naomi could not come to the Apostle Islands with me, the following summer she did go with me on an attempt to sail around Lake Huron. But the journey was short-lived. While rounding Drummond Island, we discovered that we had a large hole in the hull. The puncture had occurred in an earlier grounding in the St. Marys Channel. We had to pull in on Drummond Island and put a temporary patch on the boat so we could sail back to DeTour Village. But that's a whole 'nother adventure.

From Raspberry Island, we sailed on.

"What island is that?" I asked.

"That must be Oak Island," Naomi said, studying the map.

While we passed the island, another sailboat was on an opposite tack, coming from the east. Our paths converged and we ended up sailing on the same tack in the west channel. We sailed alongside each other while a fair breeze came up. Both boats were now moving nicely through the water. Naomi and I were gaining, slightly ahead. Suddenly, what at first been a chance meeting, turned into an impromptu race. The other boat was probably about a 32-foot sloop. We could see the crew on the other sailboat. They were busily working their sails to get every bit of forward motion possible. Naomi and I were doing the same.

"I think they're gaining on us," I told Naomi, adjusting the main sheet.

"Tighten up that jib," I ordered, excitedly. "What a day this is. A beautiful summer day, sailing into Bayfield, Wisconsin—the sailboat capital of Lake Superior."

Naomi was excited, as we raced the other boat. Then the wind picked up even more and our catamaran leaped ahead, one side of our boat came almost completely out of the water.

"Lean out," I shouted.

As we burst ahead, we were now steadily moving away from our competitors. Their boat was leaning over so far. Like us, they were giving it everything they could. But still, Naomi and I continued to widen the distance in our little $650 sailboat.

Nearing Bayfield, I spotted a nice place to land on a pebbly beach between a park and a kayak outfitters shop. We had won the race. We left the hot shot sailors in the other sailboat behind us, shame-faced. Pulling up on the pebbly beach with our beautiful little red, white and blue sailboat. Its colorful sails were flying in the wind. I don't think a peacock could have been prouder. We were explorers, racers and adventurers all in one.

CHAPTER 29
BAYFIELD

Bayfield is a beautiful place. On any warm summer day, the town is bustling with tourists, sailors and boaters all taking advantage of the weather. Naomi and I changed our clothes and secured the boat. Then we walked into town, excited as two kids heading to the candy store. We walked toward the town's main street and found a restaurant that served food on an outside deck.

"How about if we eat here?" I asked.

"Yeah, let's eat out on the deck," Naomi suggested.

After being outdoors for most of our trip, it made us almost claustrophobic to go inside and eat, especially on a beautiful day like this. After eating a fish dinner, we took a stroll through the town and checked out all the tourist gift shops and bookstores. We felt like tourists. But in our hearts, we knew we were more than that. We were sailing around Lake Superior, the first father-daughter duo to attempt this feat on a 16-foot catamaran. And now, we knew we were in the home stretch.

After touring the town and picking up a few items, we made our way back to the boat and we started re-packing our supplies. While we were doing this, a couple of young ladies stopped by to talk to us. They were curious about our boat. We visited with them for a while and told them that we were on our way around Lake Superior and talked about some of our adventures along the way.

"Where is your support team?" they asked.

"There is no support team," we answered.

"No support team?" they repeated in disbelief.

"That's right. Naomi and I are on our own. There is no outside help." They stopped and thought about that for a moment.

"That's amazing," they said.

We finished getting the boat ready and said goodbye to Bayfield and then set sail.

"We'll camp tonight on one of the islands," I said.

"Sounds good to me, Dad."

I pointed to a forest of ship masts in the harbor and said, "Let's get a few pictures of the sailboats."

"That's more sailboats than I've ever seen," Naomi said, clicking the camera.

"We'll sail until just before dark, then find a place to camp," I said.

We sailed to Long Island. There we found a sandy shore to camp on for the night and set up camp and we crawled into the tent.

"I'm going to read my new book," I told Naomi.

"What's it about, Dad?"

"It's about shipwrecks of the Apostle Islands. It's called 'The Unholy Apostles.' By James M. Keller."

I flipped the book open and glanced at the photos.

"Here's an interesting story. Want me to read it to you? It's about the schooner *Moonlight*, one of the last great sailing schooners on the lakes."

"Yeah. Sure, Dad. Read it to me."

As I read, we learned that the *Moonlight* now lies on the bottom of Lake Superior about 12 miles east of Michigan Island. The once proud schooner had set all kinds of sailing records in her heyday. Perhaps reminded of our adventure earlier in the afternoon, one story about the schooner particularly caught my interest. The *Moonlight* was once in an impromptu race with another boat called the *Porter*.

The captains of the two boats were leaving Buffalo, N.Y. for Milwaukee, Wis. at the same time. Dennis Sullivan was the captain of the *Moonlight*. He challenged *Porter* Captain Orval Green to race. Green accepted.

News of the challenge was telegraphed ahead. The race gained quite a lot of attention. At points along the way spectators watched the two schooners remain remarkably close. When they sailed through Lake Michigan, a storm erupted. Sullivan, known to sail through lots of bad weather, uncharacteristically decided to seek shelter at Port Washington.

"Ah-ha," Green thought. "This is my chance to win the race."

The next day, as the *Moonlight* sailed into Milwaukee and the crew saw the *Porter* being towed in by a tugboat with its masts and spars gone. The harbor tugs had found the *Porter* drifting helplessly after the gale. The two captains met at the dock and shook hands. They considered the race a tie then they then headed down to the bar together to discuss the race results.

The *Moonlight,* once a mighty Great Lakes schooner, eventually passed her prime. She no longer graced the lake with her sails. *Moonlight* had been reduced to a tow barge by the time she met her demise in a gale off Michigan Island. Her seams split open and she began to sink. The steamer *Volunteer* was able to rescue the crew. Today, the *Moonlight* is a piece of Great Lakes history that lies in Superior's depths for divers to enjoy.

Our eyelids were growing heavy as we closed the book.

"That was interesting Pop," said Naomi, blowing out the candle.

We said a short prayer of thanks for safe travel and the beautiful day.

"Goodnight, Dad."

"Goodnight, Naomi. I love you."

Little did I realize, as we drifted off to sleep, that I had just been inspired to write a new song called "Three Sheets to the Wind."

Three Sheets To The Wind
By Carl Behrend

Porter and the Moonlight
Were sailing ships they say
Upbound for Milwaukee out of Buffalo they say
Two captains of the finest ships
The lakes had ever seen
One was Captain Sullivan, the other Captain Green
The captain of the Moonlight challenged Captain Green
The Captain of the Porter said, "I'll race and I will win"
" I'll race and I will win so let the race begin"
They were running, they were running with the wind

They sailed across Lake Michigan, early mornin' rain
Those ships were neck and neck that day
Neither one could gain
Northwest storm began to blow, the Moonlight sailed for land
The Porter sailed into the storm, catch me if you can
Catch me if you can, I'll sail this race and win
They were running, they were running with the wind

Lightning flashed, the skies turned black
The Porter she did roll
The captain shouted orders out: "Pull down some sail"
Before the crew could do their part, they heard an awful sound

The north wind caught hold of them sails, tore them all down

They were three sheets to the wind
Will they ever make it home again?
They were running, they were running with the wind

The captain of the Moonlight waited out the storm
Anchored at Port Washington, 'till the storm was o'er
Sailed for Milwaukee, the Porter hove in sight
A tugboat towed her into port
Her masts and spars were gone

They were three sheets to the wind
Will they ever make it home again?
They were running, they were running with the wind

Two captains of the finest ships
The lakes had ever seen
One was Captain Sullivan
The other, Captain Green
The captains shook hands at the dock
We'll call the race a tie, we'll tell the tale down at the bar
O'er a few drinks, bye and bye

They were three sheets to the wind
Will they ever make it home again?
They were running, they were running with the wind

CHAPTER 30
PORCUPINE MOUNTAINS

Early the next morning, we woke up to the sound of a steady wind. We gathered our gear together and got the boat ready to sail.

"I'm going to put a reef in the mainsail," I said.

Naomi tied her things onto the boat.

"If this wind picks up any more, we could be in trouble," I said. "Let's shove off."

Another day's adventure had begun.

While we passed the Long Island Lighthouse, we wondered how many ships she had seen pass by. How many stories could that lighthouse tell?

"It sure looks beautiful in the morning sun," Naomi said.

"Get a picture," I told her as we moved slowly past. "What a great life we have."

Naomi snapped her pictures.

"How many people get to do this? Sail around Lake Superior?" I wondered, as we sailed to the east. Later that morning, the winds calmed to almost nothing. We started our trusty outboard motor and kept going. By early afternoon, the sun had started shining brightly. We were both ready for a little break.

We pulled the boat in at Little Girls Point. There was a pebbly beach at the mouth of a small river. A family of tourists who were enjoying the beach welcomed us and they shared their lunch with us while we shared stories of our adventure.

"I'm going for a swim," I said.

I grabbed my snorkel and fins. Naomi got out shampoo to wash her hair. It was a great summer day and the waters of Lake Superior were the best place to be enjoying it. We lay in the sun on the beach for a while. Then we climbed back on the boat again and sailed toward the Porcupine Mountains.

"I must say, this is one of the most enjoyable days we've had," I said.

The calm seas made for easy motoring. The Porcupine Mountains stayed in the distance for a long time. After riding for hours, we still hadn't reached them.

"You know how everything is farther than you think on this lake, Dad."

"Yeah, I know."

Finally, as evening approached, we found the shoreline at Porcupine Mountains State Park. Thinking about the mountains reminded me of a phone call I had received some time back from Don Hermanson, a friend of mine from Keweenaw Video Productions. There was a sense of urgency in his voice. He said, "Carl, I'm making a video about the Porcupine Mountains State Park. I need a song about the Porcupine Mountains. But I need it right away." He said he would send me a script to see if I could write a song for the video. The telephone call had come on a Tuesday. I received the script on Thursday when I checked the mailbox after work.

Naomi was home from school. She had worked with me that day. She was cooking supper while I read through a couple of pages of the script. I had been on a few camping trips to the "Porkies" before. I had some knowledge of the area. I put the script down and almost joking, I picked up my guitar and spontaneously blurted out the first words that came to my head: "Traveling north to the Porcupine Mountains. Porcupine Mountains, by Superior's sea . . ."

"Hey, that sounded pretty good," Naomi yelled from the kitchen.

"Yeah, I think I'll write it down."

Supper was ready. So I put it down the guitar to go and eat. After supper, I went to play hockey so I didn't have a chance to work on the song it that evening. But the next morning, I got up early and was able to finish it. I was excited as I called Don.

"Your song is ready," I said.

"How does it go?" he said, surprised I'd finished already.

I got my guitar. I held the phone to my cheek with my shoulder.

"I'll sing it for you over the phone. Here it goes:

Travelin' north to the Porcupine Mountains.
Porcupine Mountains, by Superior's sea
And when I reach them Porcupine Mountains
That's when I know that I am really free

Hiking the trails of the Porcupine Mountains
Lake of the Clouds inspires me

And I hear the falls of Mana'b'oozoo
I can hear that Great Spirit speak to me

Your lofty trees, your rolling mountains, your great and shining sea
Has brought me back to the Porcupine Mountains; Porcupine
Mountains, by Superior, shining sea

Summer days change into autumn
And the trees are red and gold
I'll tell your tales by the firelight
Like the Indians back in the days of old

Winter comes upon the mountains
And the snows fall white and deep
I will roam across your mountains
'Cross your mountains and your valleys on my skis

Your lofty trees and rolling mountains, your great and shining sea
Has brought me back to the Porcupine Mountains; Porcupine
Mountains, by Superior's shining sea

Travelin' north, to the Porcupine Mountains.
Porcupine Mountains, by Superior's sea
And when I reach them Porcupine Mountains
That's when I know that I am really free
That's when I know that I am really free

When I was finished, Don said, "Sounds good. Can you come up this weekend and record it?"

"Sure."

That's how my "Porcupine Mountains Wilderness Song" came to be on the state park video. Naomi and I now sang the song as we floated past the mountain range. We admired the beautiful scenery. The golden hues of evening reflected on the water giving warmth to the rocks and forests along the shore. A slight breeze lifted up. The wind moved the boat forward. One of us said, "Shut that noisy thing off," talking about the boat motor. I pulled the propeller out of the water.

Nothing makes a sailor happier than when he can shut off the boat motor and sail away. A nice breeze pushed us past the campground at Union Bay. The sounds of the campers rose from the shoreline.

"We'll pull up on that sand beach over there," I said.

A couple greeted us who had been watching our boat from the shore.

"A Prindle 16 with a reefed main," the man said.

"Yeah, that's right," I said.

"I used to race tornado catamarans," the man said.

He introduced himself, but I can remember his name.

"My name is Carl and this is my daughter Naomi," I said. "We're on our way around Lake Superior."

"That's great," he said, looking at our gear strapped to the boat. He helped us pull the boat to shore. The couple sat and talked to us while we made camp. They helped us gather wood for a fire.

"We're Great Lakes balladeers," I said.

We cooked supper over the fire.

"My song is on the Porcupine Mountains State Park video. We'll sing a couple of songs for you after supper," I said.

The sun sank over the lake. The colors of the sky were more glorious than I had ever remembered. In the darkness, we all sat up by the campfire. Naomi and I serenaded our visitors well into the night. The campfire glowed under the warm summer sky. With the lapping of the waves keeping time to the music, it was another perfect evening on the shores of Lake Superior.

CHAPTER 31
FOURTEEN MILE POINT

Morning found us up early and busily breaking camp. We loaded the boat and were sailing early. We shoved off from the beautiful sand beach at Union Bay. It was one of the most pleasant places we stayed on our whole trip.

The breeze freshened and began to move us steadily on our way. What adventures would we have today? What interesting experiences were waiting? Those were the kind of thoughts we had as we began each day. We approached each day with a sense of wonder. Lake Superior has a way of doing that to you.

The winds increased. We were soon scooting along at a high speed and loving every minute of it.

"This is so much better than the Minnesota side," I said.

"Yeah. These winds behind us sure make us move."

Before we knew it, we were in the middle of towering whitecaps. We surfed down the waves, feeling triumphant that we'd conquered them. At the same time, we questioned ourselves as to what kind of fools we were to be several miles out in Lake Superior with waves like this.

We were both a little scared.

But we were both hollering, "Yippee!"

We yelled each time we surfed down the back of another giant wave. It didn't take long for us to blow by Ontonagon with a tremendous following sea. We were then on to Fourteen Mile Point.

"When we get to Fourteen Mile Point, I want to stop and look at the lighthouse," I told Naomi.

The old lighthouse belonged to a friend of ours from Houghton. Within sight of Fourteen Mile Point, one of the most tragic shipwrecks of the lake took place. The final voyage of the *St. Clair* began on July 7, 1876. Stopping at Bayfield, Ashland and Ontonagon, she left Ontonagon about 11:55 p.m. on July 8 with a load of freight and livestock. The weather was calm. The ship made good time. By 1:35 a.m., the *St. Clair* was off Fourteen Mile Point. The chief engineer checked the engine room before retiring for the night, when he thought he smelled smoke and discovered a raging fire in the hold. He sounded the alarm. The ship's crew fought the fire. But the blaze spread through the vessel and quickly destroyed the ship's yawl.

Meanwhile, the captain remembered a lifeboat was in the cargo hold, which was to be delivered to Houghton. With great difficulty, the lifeboat was launched as it was dropped into the water. Captain Rynas was knocked overboard. Climbing back onto the small boat, he helped bring it alongside the burning ship. He then helped 12 passengers into the boat. One passenger leapt from an upper deck, capsizing the lifeboat. In the chaos that followed, other passengers began to leap. This caused the lifeboat to roll over and over.

When the tiny boat was finally righted, only three men: Captain Rynas, the chief engineer, and passenger J.B. Stotphin—who later became mayor of Duluth—were bailing water and picking up other survivors. A wheelman and a mate were found on a floating hatch cover. With only one oar, the men had to use the lifeboat seats as paddles. One man died on the way to shore. Another suffered heart failure, but was revived. The weary survivors took about seven hours to finally reach the home of a fisherman near Portage Entry. Of the 31 passengers and crew, only five survived. The captain found the tug *Bob Anderson*, which returned to the scene. Only 14 bodies were recovered.

The Fourteen Mile Lighthouse was architecturally one of the most elaborate lighthouses. Vandals burned the building on July 30, 1984. It was a terrible loss. The building had remained mostly intact until that time.

Naomi and I had a rather difficult time making our way to the rocky shore through the breaking waves. But eventually, we pulled the boat up on the rocks and we set off to explore the ruins of the lighthouse.

"What a beautiful building this must have been," Naomi lamented.

"Yeah. Look at the design of the brick work on the porch."

We wandered around the building. Even in this dilapidated condition, the lighthouse was still an awesome structure. Most of the brick walls were standing. The tower and lantern room were also intact. With this framework in place, we could visualize the original building. The fog signal building stood near the water's edge in very good condition. That building was a sad reminder of how the magnificent lighthouse could have stayed, if left unmolested.

We took some pictures.

"Should we have lunch before we go?" I asked.

"No, I've got an idea. Why don't we stop at the Superior View Restaurant in Freda?"

"Hey, that sounds like a great idea. It's probably about 15 more miles or so. With this wind, we should be there easily in an hour or two."

Eagerly, we launched our boat, saying goodbye to the lighthouse. We then headed for Freda, which was once a thriving town overlooking Lake Superior. The place was also the site of a stamp mill for processing copper ore for the Copper Range Mining Company. There were other mills located nearby including Red Ridge and Beacon Hill. But with the end of copper mining in the area, the buildings and town sites were soon left behind. Today, they are a faint glimmer of the bustling industries that thrived here when copper was king.

While we worked our way east, Naomi and I talked about what we would have for dinner. The restaurant at Freda was fashioned from an old office building at the Copper Range Stamp Mill.

We were familiar with the area from frequent visits to Naomi's grandparents. They lived nearby. Because we skipped lunch, we could hardly wait to arrive at Freda. But, wouldn't you know it, just when we thought we would have a speedy ride over there, the wind died.

"Doggone it," I said. "I'm going to have to start that blasted motor."

I went to the back of the boat. Naomi and I both disliked the noise. But we had no choice. We got the motor running and moved along at a snail's pace. We were tossed about by rolling waves. What we figured would be an hour or two ride from Fourteen Mile Point, turned into a long four-hour trip.

We finally arrived and pulled the boat up onto the sand beach. Securing the boat, we finally got ready to go to the restaurant. By then, we had both decided what we would eat. I can't remember now what I said I was going to order. But Naomi said she didn't think they would have it.

"I'll bet you five dollars they do," I said.

I turned and we started walking up the trail to Freda.

By this time, we were absolutely famished. We walked up the hill past the foundations of the old stamp mill. Finally, we got to the restaurant only to find a woman who cleaned the place tell us that they weren't open that day. We felt as though we just heard the worst news in the world. We were so disappointed.

"I guess we'll just cook something back down at the boat," I told Naomi.

Reaching the catamaran, we unpacked our gear and gathered wood for a fire.

"Even though we're disappointed about the restaurant, I still enjoy eating out here," I said.

"Yeah."

After we ate lunch. We packed up and headed for Houghton Canal. The waves on the lake had settled down some, but they were still breaking along the shore. That made launching the boat rather tricky.

"Houghton Canal, here we come," I said.

"I would love to sail around the Keweenaw Peninsula," Naomi said.

"I would too."

We meant it. There is nothing I would rather do than to spend our summers sailing around Lake Superior. But time, money and commitments always seem to interfere and obscure the possibility of taking the time for adventures like this.

I believe it was Henry David Thoreau who once said, "For want of making a living, some have never taken the time to live." How true those words rang now. It was great to be able to take a month's time away from the ordinary hustle and bustle of life. And better yet, to spend this time with my daughter out here among the most beautiful places in the world. Indeed, I felt that for the first time in my life I was really alive. Even wealthy men told me I was fortunate to be able to take a month off during the summer. I felt that somehow they envied me. Somehow, I felt that I was wealthier than they.

While we approached Portage Entry, the colors of the sunset glanced off the smooth surface of the water. We glided through it. I realized that the gold of the sunset and the valuable time I'd spent with my daughter made me far richer than many men could ever hope to imagine.

The sun was fully set. We made our way through the break walls at Portage Entry.

"I hope we can make it to Houghton before it's too dark," I said. "If we get to a phone you can call your mom."

Naomi's mother, my ex-wife Mary, lived nearby with her parents.

"I'll call Don Hermanson to see if he'll put me up for the night."

"There's a park just before the bridge," Naomi said. "There's probably a pay phone there."

We moved into the clear waters of the Portage Canal. Portage Lake is truly a wonder of nature. The crooked finger shaped lake nearly separated the Keweenaw Peninsula from the mainland. The waterway was long used by Native Americans. Later, voyagers and fur traders used the route as they traveled the lakeshore. The shortcut saved them more than a hundred miles of grueling travel around the tip of the Keweenaw. These travelers would carry their canoes and supplies from Portage Lake over the narrow isthmus to Lake Superior, thus the name "Portage Lake." A canal was dug here in the late 1800s and later widened.

We passed an old Coast Guard Station along the shore. The building reminded us of some of the daring rescues made by the Portage Lifesaving Station crews. One particular story stands out in my mind. It was the story of the Canadian steamer *Maplehurst*. In a November gale in 1922, the 230-foot steel steamer sought shelter along the Keweenaw shoreline. Twenty-nine year old captain George Menard passed up Copper Harbor, thinking the entrance was too shallow. He kept going until he neared Portage Entry. Then, about three miles from the entrance, the ship was pounded by giant waves.

Menard ordered flares lighted as a distress signal. Lifesaving Captain Charles A. Tucker and his crew boarded a motor lifeboat and were soon making their way to the troubled ship. It took about a half hour to reach the ship in the towering waves.

Meanwhile, Menard told his crew they could leave if they wished. But he would remain with the ship. As the lifeboat approached the *Maplehurst*, Captain Tucker shouted through his megaphone for the crew to jump to the lifeboat when he pulled into the lee of the vessel.

The *Maplehurst's* crew did not comply, much to the consternation of the lifesaving crew. After making ten passes, nine crewmen had made it to the lifeboat. One man, the first mate, missed the boat and drowned.

Then, a giant wave struck the *Maplehurst* and her lights went out. Unable to find the ship through darkness and blinding snow, Tucker had no choice but to go back to the lifesaving station. Eleven Canadian sailors were lost that night. The lifesavers had done what they could. The next day, only the tops of the *Maplehurst's* derricks and smokestacks were visible.

We continued as the evening grew darker. I knew our friend Don Hermanson lived somewhere near Oscar Bay. But I wasn't sure where. So we continued into Houghton. Now it was totally dark. A couple of times, we had to shine the flashlight up onto the sails so that passing boats could see and avoid a collision. We approached Houghton Canal Park and found a spot to park the boat. We were just pulling the boat up when I heard a voice in the darkness.

"Carl," the voice yelled.

"Who could it be?" I wondered. Who knew where we would be?

"Yeah," I answered.

"It's Don." the voice said.

It was Don Hermanson. He had watched us pass at Oscar Bay. He had tried to get our attention. But we had continued on. Don gave us a ride to Naomi's mother's house. We dropped her off there for the night. Then Don brought me to his house where he fed me supper. He let me sleep there that night. Although it was nice to sleep in a bed, I had grown more accustomed to sleeping in our tent along the Lake Superior shore.

CHAPTER 32
COMMERCIAL FISHERMEN

The next morning, we all met down at the boat. Don had called a friend from WLUC-TV6 News who met with us there too. The reporter interviewed Naomi and I while we loaded our gear onto the boat. We got the sails ready to go. Don had his video camera out too. He shot some footage of our boat.

I had met Don a few years earlier while he was filming a video about the Seul Choix Point Lighthouse. He asked me if he could use my song "Ballad of Seul Choix Point Lighthouse" on the video.

"We'll need to get a professional recording," he told me.

He sent me to a studio that did a fine job recording me. Through the years, Don has been one of the most influential people helping to guide my music career. He owns Keweenaw Video Productions. He is also a filmmaker who has made a series of documentary videos about Great Lakes lighthouses. Now, here he was again helping us promote our trip around the lake.

Naomi and I were ready to launch. We said our goodbyes and off we went. There was a very strong wind from the northwest that propelled our boat ahead nicely.

"Keep an eye on the top of the mast," I yelled to Naomi while we headed for the Houghton Lift Bridge. We had called the bridge operator earlier and asked if we would need the bridge lifted for our 32-foot mast. He said he didn't think so.

But we were still concerned. We got closer to the bridge. Finally, the operator shouted to us. "You'll clear by a couple of feet," he said, reassuring us. I sheeted in the main sail and I shouted to Naomi to tighten up the jib. We were off like a rocket.

"These winds couldn't be any better," I told Naomi.

We sailed past downtown Houghton and an old stamp mill on the other side of Portage Lake. "Let's get a few pictures," Naomi suggested. This time, we both took a few photos. It was a beautiful morning. The skies were blue. We were both in high spirits. A larger sailboat closely followed us through the ship canal and down to Chassel Bay.

When we hit the more open waters in the bay, our boat leaped ahead with such force I yelled to Naomi to lean out. We both bent out over the water so the boat could take as much wind as possible without capsizing.

"We'll have to pull in somewhere when we reach the South Portage Entry," I shouted over the sound of the wind and waves. The hulls of our boat churned through the water like those of a powerboat. The sailboat that followed us, grew smaller and smaller. We shot ahead through 3-foot waves.

"If the waves are this big on Portage Lake, I wonder how big they are on the big lake?" I asked.

"Yeah. They must be huge."

We splashed along. By this time, the sailboat was completely out of sight. We held onto the boat as tight as we could. We soon reached the South Portage Entry. That 20-mile distance from Houghton was probably the fastest travel of our entire voyage.

"We're flying," Naomi said.

We pulled into a small park near the entry.

"We'll reef the main sail and lash everything down real good," I said. "It's going to be real rough out on the big lake."

"Okay, Pop."

We busily prepared for Lake Superior.

Don told us that the distance from South Portage Entry to Point Abbaye, across Keweenaw Bay, was about 20 miles. Don would know. He had fished many times with his father, growing up. His dad was an Oskar Bay commercial fisherman. But like members of so many other fishing families on the Great Lakes, Don's dad had long since retired his boats and nets. His story, and the stories of many other old commercial fishing families, inspired me to write this song:

The Great Lakes Fisherman
By Carl Behrend

Fished these waters all my life
Support six kids and a loving wife
Like my Dad and my brother Slim
I am a Great Lakes fisherman

The waves are rough. The wind is cold

I feel a longing down in my soul
If I make it back to the harbor tonight
You know everything's going to be all right

But tonight he strums his mandolin
His music's playin' in the wind
He'll laugh and sing with his old friends
But in the morning he's back on his boat again

But his hands are cold and he's getting old
There's no where else to go
His hands are cold and he's getting old
There's nowhere else to go

Early morn' before the break of day
He loads his nets, sails away
Catch seems smaller every day
This old job ain't worth the pay

Some days he thinks of giving up
Work behind a desk or driving truck
But in the end, it always goes
That catching fish is all he knows

But his hands are cold and he's getting old
There's no where else to go
His hands are cold and he's getting old
There's nowhere else to go

But tonight he strums his mandolin
His music's playin' in the wind
He'll laugh and sing with his old friends
But in the morning he's back on his boat again

But his hands are cold and he's getting old
There's no where else to go
His hands are cold and he's getting old
There's nowhere else to go

Breaking ice all out of the bay
Broke a rudder just the other day
They'll be breaking ice on their way back in
God bless the Great Lakes fisherman

But tonight he strums his mandolin
Those cold old hands come alive again
He'll laugh and sing with his old friends
But in the morning he's back on his boat again

But his hands are cold and he's getting old
There's no where else to go
His hands are cold and he's getting old
There's nowhere else to go

The first time Don heard that song I had stopped by his office in Houghton. I asked him if he would like to hear some new songs I'd written. When he said he would, I got my guitar out and played him a couple. Then I told him I had a new one about the Great Lakes commercial fishermen. He listened quietly as I played. I repeated the lines at the end of the song:

His hands are cold
He's getting old
But there's nowhere else to go

I looked up at Don. I thought I saw him wipe a tear from his eye.

CHAPTER 33
THE HURON ISLANDS

Sailing southwest, we passed the Portage Entry Lighthouse. We set a course for Point Abbaye. We knew it was going to be rough out on the open lake. But with the winds almost directly behind us, the boat sailed nicely over the waves.

With the South Portage Entry lighthouse getting smaller behind us the protection from the waves grew less and less, until finally we were in monstrous waves. But by now, Naomi and I felt quite immune to danger. We were actually enjoying our situation.

"I wish that we had time to stop and visit our relatives along Keweenaw Bay," I said. "But if we don't make it back for mom and dad's 50th wedding anniversary, they'll disown us."

Naomi said, "There's so many places I'd like to sail to. But it's already August 6. We better keep going."

So on we sailed over the mountainous waves. We were in high spirits. In what seemed to be no time at all, we were rounding Point Abbaye. Looming up before us, lay the Huron Islands. At first they looked like small blue mounds on the surface of the water. But as the winds blew us steadily closer, the islands seemed to grow out of the horizon.

"Dad, is that the lighthouse I see there?"

"No, I don't think so."

It had been many years since I visited the lighthouse on Huron Island. I couldn't remember how everything looked.

"My Dad brought us out here when I was about 12 years old," I said. "I see a building, but I don't see a lighthouse."

We moved nearer and could see that the structure was a fog signal building.

"I'm not sure where the lighthouse is," I said, somewhat puzzled. "Maybe something happened to it."

Then, as we rounded the northwest point of the island, Naomi said, "Is that it?"

She pointed to a high rocky cliff in the middle of the island.

"Yeah. That's it," I said, excitedly. "I was worried something had happened to it, like the lighthouse at Fourteen Mile Point."

"Now, where are we going to land, Dad?"

"We'll pull up in the lee wind side of the island. We couldn't land anywhere on the other side in these waves."

High above the blue water sat the Huron Island Lighthouse.

"It's even more beautiful than I had remembered," I said.

The island is made up of huge granite rocks whose colors, I believe, are the most beautiful in Lake Superior. It was rather treacherous landing the boat. But somehow, Naomi and I always managed.

"This is awesome, Dad."

We climbed the rocky cliff to the lighthouse. The view was majestic.

"I think this is one of the most beautiful places we have stopped. At least on the U.S. side. Maybe our entire trip," I said.

We clicked more pictures of the lighthouse and surrounding scenery. Next to the lighthouse was another building. This structure was likely built later for Coast Guard personnel to use, back when the lighthouse was still manned.

"Hey, Naomi! Here's a trail that goes to the fog signal building."

"Let's hike down there, Pop."

We went down the path to the north end of the island. We wanted to see what new discoveries waited for us there. The whole island was beautiful. The lighthouse and fog signal building gave us plenty to explore. The fog signal building was still quite intact as we looked around inside. We felt as though we were seeing history come alive.

In a 1909 storm, two ships were lost near here. They were the 291-foot wooden steamer *Iosco* and the 242-foot schooner barge *Olive Jeanette*. In a September 3 storm, the two boats were perhaps seeking the shelter of the Keweenaw waterway. The *Iosco* must have gone down first as the ships fought a losing battle. Debris from the wrecks showed up along the shoreline all the way from the Huron Mountains to Keweenaw Bay. Many people on the mainland wondered what had happened.

Then on September 5, the keeper of the Huron Island Light completed a 20-mile rowing trip to Pequaming. He reported that he had watched a schooner sink about four miles north of the lighthouse. The light keeper saw no steamer in sight when he watched the waterlogged schooner make her final plunge. Whatever caused both ships to sink remains a mystery. There were no survivors to tell the story.

Naomi and I made our way back to the lighthouse, where we found another trail.

"I wonder where this goes?" I said.

Naomi, always one for adventure, said, "Let's go find out."

So off we went again to the other end of the island, enjoying the beautiful scenery and taking photos as we went. At the end of the path was a small harbor with a dock and a boathouse.

"I don't remember this," I told Naomi. "But when I came here with my Dad this must be where we parked the boat."

It was the only protected spot on the island to keep a boat. On the way back to the catamaran, we took a shortcut and found some nice patches of blueberries. We stopped and picked some.

"There's nothing like fresh blueberries," I said.

"Yeah."

We ate the berries by the handful.

These islands must have been a wild place back in 1860, before there was a lighthouse or a foghorn. That year, a group of mariners found themselves alone in the fog on the night of May 28. The 237-foot sidewheel steamer *Arctic* slammed aground on the south end of the island. Fortunately, the passengers and crew were able to jump from the bow to the shore before rising seas destroyed the wooden ship. The boat was carrying a cargo of dishes and plates.

By now, the sun was coming out again. The wind had died down. We prepared to shove off.

"I'd like to come back here again," I said.

"Me too."

We pushed away from the huge rocks

"It would be nice to camp here for a few days," Naomi said.

We took one last look at the beautiful rocks and the lighthouse towering over the rocky cliff.

"Well, it's off to Big Bay," I said.

We set sail under a rather light breeze. We had gone for about an hour when I decided to start the motor. We cruised along lazily as the lake calmed to a rolling sea.

"Those are the Huron Mountains," I told Naomi.

Back in the early 1900s, a group of wealthy businessmen bought much of the land there and formed The Huron Mountain Club. The club members were only the most elite.

"Henry Ford spent most of his time there," I said. "He had that beautiful house in Pequaming and it was hardly ever used."

I looked at Naomi.

"We used to go camping near the mouth of the Huron River when the kids were small. It was such a beautiful spot with sand beaches and the Huron Islands in the distance."

"I think I remember that," Naomi said.

"I don't think so, you weren't born yet. But, Caleb and Sarah might remember."

After a few hours motoring, we found ourselves near a huge rocky cliff.

"I think Big Bay is right around there," I said.

"I hope so, Dad. Those storm clouds are moving in on us and they look mighty nasty."

"Yeah. I know. I've been watching them too. If we can make it around that cliff, I think we'll be all right."

The air was dead calm. But to the west of us, the storm was closing in. If I could have gone any faster, I would have. But our little boat just sputtered along. This added to our worry and the suspense of the moment. Would we make it before the storm hit? I wondered, as we pressed on.

Just as we rounded the point into Big Bay, it seemed like all hell broke loose.

"Batten down the hatches," I yelled. "Pull down the jib."

Suddenly, a strong wind hit us like a ton of bricks from somewhere back in the approaching thunder. The motor came popping out of the water. The boat was now going faster than the motor could handle. I shut off the engine and held onto the steering tiller.

"Is that a water spout over there?" Naomi yelled.

We catapulted ahead at an incredible speed.

"All we can do is hang on," I shouted.

The forward motion of the boat reminded me of one of those iceboats. Faster and faster we went. The rain began pelting us. Lightning and thunder crashed all around us. To the right of us was a stonewall cliff with no place to land. We rocketed ahead. The wind nearly lifted us out of the water. We blew closer toward the beach at the end of the bluff.

"Hang on! We're going to crash," I yelled.

The force of the wind thrust us to the shore and about 20 feet up onto the beach. Finally, we stopped.

"Turn her into the wind," I hollered over the wild flapping of the sails.

We struggled to move the boat on dry ground. The rain was coming down in torrents. We dropped the sail and grabbed our packs.

"Let's run for the road," I said.

Just as we got there, a set of headlights appeared. Apparently, the two people inside the car were watching the storm out over the lake when they saw us.

"Can we catch a ride to town?" I yelled.

"Jump in," said the man behind the wheel.

"Bring us to the Thunder Bay Inn," I said.

We drove off in the pouring rain.

"I can't believe you were out in that storm," the man said.

"We can't either," we told him.

"We saw a water spout forming," Naomi said.

We arrived at the inn. The people in the car were Fred and Rita Buser. They said they camped in the area every summer and they really enjoyed it. We thanked them for the ride while we unloaded our backpacks from the car.

"Just another part of the adventure," I told Naomi.

We tramped into the inn. We must have been quite a sight in our wetsuits and rain gear. Our hair was wet and matted. Our faces were sunburned and wind whipped. We were carrying our orange waterproof dry bags on our backs. We were all dripping wet.

"We don't look like your average tourists," I thought, as we made our way through the dining room to the front desk. After hot showers and a whitefish dinner, I decided to entertain a few of the guests in the lounge. I took out my backpacker's guitar. It was another perfect ending to another wonderful day.

CHAPTER 34

HOMEWARD BOUND

Naomi and I were again up early. Someone from the inn gave us a ride down to the lake. It took us a while to get the boat ready. We had to push it all the way back down to the water after the storm had blown us high and dry.

"That was some storm, last night, Hey, Dad?"

We were setting the sails for another day's journey.

"Yeah. That was pretty nasty. It's a good thing we made it around that point and got some protection from those cliffs, or it might have been a different story. We'll be on the home stretch now."

Shoving off into the cold lake, I told Naomi, "We could make it home to Munising today."

"Well today is August 7. We have until the 8th. That's when grandma and grandpa are having their anniversary party," Naomi said.

"Yeah. And I'm already the black sheep. But it looks like we'll make it."

We steered our boat out of Big Bay and into the open waters of Lake Superior.

"It looks like it's going to be a nice day," Naomi said.

She tightened the jib.

"That certainly was a welcomed stop," I said.

Just then, a nice breeze came up that pushed us on our way. It wasn't long before we passed the Big Bay Point Lighthouse. As usual, I told Naomi to take a couple of pictures. The lighthouse looked beautiful in the morning sun.

"What a great day to be sailing on Lake Superior," I said, blissfully. "I'm going to hate to see it end."

Naomi kept shooting the camera.

The Big Bay Lighthouse was built in 1868. The beacon is still an active light. The brick design of the building is similar to that of the Fourteen Mile Point Lighthouse. For a time, the area was used as an anti-aircraft artillery range. Today, the lighthouse is privately owned and is now a bed and breakfast inn.

"That was cool Pop.

"Not many people have seen as many lighthouses as we have."

"That's true. And from the water besides."

We sailed on in a fair breeze, making good time. But despite our speed, we were having a relaxing sail.

"It doesn't get much better than this," I said.

"Is that Granot Loma?" Naomi asked.

She was pointing to a big log cabin along the shore.

"No, that was his brother's place."

I was referring to Louis Kaufman's brother.

"Granot Loma is up around the point here, a little ways. It's the Taj Mahal of log cabins, built in the 30s for the wealthy banker and renowned Marquette businessman Louis G. Kaufman."

It is said that Kaufman built Granot Loma after not being able to join the Huron Mountain Club because he was Jewish. So he went and built his own lodge. The original estate included many square miles of forest and some of the most fantastic lakeshore property on Lake Superior.

Granot Loma overlooks a small island named Saukshead Island. The story is often told that a group of Sauk warriors was traveling west when they were discovered by a band of Chippewas. A battle ensured. The victorious Chippewas placed the impaled heads of their fallen foes on sticks along the shoreline of this small island. That horrific visual warning was meant as a deterrent for any more hostile Indians who might paddle their canoes this way. The Chippewa and the Sauk had at one time been brothers. They shared a common language. But a blood feud arose that lasted all the way into the mid 1800s. The Sauk were allies with the Sioux.

Soon we were passing Granot Loma.

"That's Granot Loma," I told Naomi.

"Oh, wow. That is huge," Naomi said.

"I've been inside it too," I told her. "It's really awesome."

I tried to describe some of the outstanding features to her.

Soon we could see the city of Marquette in the distance. The territory was becoming more and more familiar.

"Look at that island," Naomi said, as we sailed closer to Marquette. "What island is that? Is that a lighthouse?"

"Yeah. That's Granite Island Lighthouse."

"Should we sail out to it?"

"No, it's too far out of our way. Besides, I heard the island is covered with bird poop."

"Eee yew!"

Naomi wrinkled her nose.

The Granite Island Light was built the same year as the Big Bay Point Lighthouse. Like the Big Bay beacon, the Granite Island Light is still an active light and has been sold to a private party. The owners are working on restoring the lighthouse.

We continued past Presque Isle and the Upper Harbor of Marquette.

"We'll pull in by the Marquette Harbor lighthouse and take a little break," I told Naomi.

There was a beautiful little cove just west of the lighthouse with a sandy beach. Naomi and I pulled up there, next to the lighthouse. The Marquette Harbor Light was built in 1866. The structure is a square brick building that reminds you of a castle. As a matter of fact, I've heard it said that lighthouses are the "castles of America." That's why preserving them is so important.

"Let's walk over to the maritime museum," I said. "I sold them a bunch of CDs before we left and I told Jerry Wiater about our upcoming trip. He'll be surprised to see that we actually made it around the lake."

The Marquette Harbor has a rich history of Great Lakes shipping and the maritime museum does a fine job presenting that history. Jerry Wiater was in charge of running the museum. So we stopped in for a visit. We even brought our backpacker's guitar and played a few tunes while in the museum.

Jerry was so impressed. He had to come down to the beach to see our boat. He asked a lot of questions about the catamaran and our voyage. He seemed to be wishing he were taking the same kind of trip himself.

"Well, this is the last part of our trip," we told him.

"We'll be back in Munising sometime tonight," I said.

Just before packing up, some folks on the beach asked me to play Gordon Lightfoot's *Wreck of the Edmund Fitzgerald*. So we did and then topped it off with *What Do You Do With a Drunken Sailor?* The people on the beach all laughed and wished us well. We then shoved off on the final leg of our voyage.

Sailing east, we set a course for Shot Point, leaving the bright red lighthouse and the Coast Guard buildings behind. Before the Coast Guard, the Lifesaving Service handled the duties of aiding boats and ships in distress. They say the Marquette lifesaving crew was the best-trained team in the country. The crew won all kinds of recognition. At the height of their fame, Captain Henry Cleary and his lifesaving crew attended expositions all across the country. Most notably, they were at the 1893 Chicago World's Fair.

At one of these expositions, the Indian Chief Geronimo was a frequent visitor to the lifesaving exhibit. Perhaps, there was a kindred spirit felt between the old warrior and the "storm warriors," as they were called.

One of the Marquette crew's most daring rescues began on the stormy morning of Sept. 29, 1895. The wooden steamer *Charles J. Kershaw* was struggling to reach the harbor with the schooner barges *Kent* and *Moonlight* (the same *Moonlight* mentioned earlier). The *Kershaw* broke a steam pipe, losing power. The ships were driven southeastward toward the dreaded Chocolay Reef. The two schooners missed striking the reef. But the gale pushed them onto the beach so high that they were nearly on dry land.

The *Kershaw* wasn't so lucky. She caught on the reef and was pounded mercilessly by the surf. A lifesaving patrol spotted the wreck at 2:45 a.m. It took a miserable four hours work to drag the lifesavers' surfboat through sand, brush and mud to a site near the wreck.

Captain Cleary and his brave crew launched through the waves. They came up alongside the *Kershaw*. They were only able to take nine of the crew onboard as they rowed for shore. The boat capsized, injuring one of the lifesavers. Cleary immediately called for a volunteer to take the injured lifesaver's place. Then he set out for the stricken steamer once more. But just before the lifesavers reached the ship, three giant waves capsized the lifeboat. The rescue party was washed ashore. The lifeboat was now damaged beyond repair. Three more lifesavers were injured with four more desperate sailors at rescue. Cleary returned to the station for another lifeboat.

Once again, with the help of three more volunteers, he made his way to the wreck. By now, the *Kershaw* was breaking up. The wary captain and his three men huddled in the ship's yawl. This time, they successfully removed the remaining sailors. Cleary used a drag and was able to make it to safety without capsizing. This was one of the most dramatic local rescues and it was witnessed by thousands of Marquette citizens. The *Kershaw* was a total loss. As for the *Moonlight* and *Kent*, they spent the entire winter on the beach at Chocolay. They were re-floated in the spring, reportedly at enormous cost.

Naomi and I continued our homeward journey around Shot Point. By now, the wind had died down and we were running the motor again. When we got between Shelter Bay and AuTrain Island, I noticed something was wrong.

"This boat is moving awfully slow," I said.

"What do you think is wrong, Pop?"

I grumbled.

"I'm not sure, but this boat is acting sluggish,"

I went to the back of the boat to check the rudders.

"What the heck?"

The back of the boat was underwater, practically drowning the motor.

"What's wrong, Dad?"

Naomi had a worried look in her face.

"We're sinking. Stay to the front of the boat and help keep the motor out of the water. We'll head for AuTrain Island. That's the nearest land. I must have forgotten to put the hull plug back in."

After what seemed like forever, we arrived at AuTrain Island. I nosed the boat ashore on a rock beach.

"Sure enough. The boat is full of water," I said, inspecting the catamaran. "Let's pull the boat up as far as we can. Then I'll show you some caves."

"That would be cool Pop."

We heaved with all our strength.

Leaving the boat to drain, we headed to the caves. When we got there, I climbed into one and disappeared. Naomi wondered what happened to me.

"Dad, where are you?"

What she didn't know was that the cave came out on the other side of the cliff. Circling behind her, I made a growling noise.

"Grrrrrr!"

"Ooooh," Naomi shrieked.

Then she could hear me laughing.

"The cave goes all the way through," I said.

I pointed to the opening.

"That is so cool."

"Stick with your old Pop and you'll learn a thing or two."

This time, we both went into the cave and out the other side.

"Well, let's get back to the boat," I said.

We walked back down to the lake. The sun was setting. The colors of evening painted the sky. We talked as we drained the last bit of water out of the hull.

"Well, should we stay here tonight, or should we go into Munising?" I asked.

"In a way, I'm eager to get back and in another way I would love to camp out here by the lake another night."

"I feel the same way. I'm anxious to get back and tell everyone we made it. Yet, the lake seems to be beckoning us to stay another night. I guess we're this close we might as well go home. We'll have things to do before grandma and grandpa's party."

We put the hull plug in. The lake was very calm now. So we made our way back over the last remaining miles. We were happy to be getting closer to home and sad to be leaving the lake that we had come to love. No wonder they call her "Superior." No other name would fit her. No other name would do.

It was dark now. We headed into Munising past Five Mile Point. In the darkness we could make out the shapes of Wood Island and Williams Island. I once spent two weeks on Williams Island, working on the only cabin out there.

"Naomi, do you remember the time you kids helped me on that cabin?"

"Yeah. That was awesome."

We passed the island then headed into the west channel. Like an old friend, Grand Island was waiting for us. Passing the island, we slipped into the cold waters of Munising Bay. The lights of the town guided us in.

"We'll pull in by the marina," I told Naomi. I headed the boat for Munising city dock. "There's a phone there we can use."

I planned to call my fiancé Dori or my son Caleb to come and pick us up. It was 1:30 a.m., August 8 when we finally set foot on land. There was no reception committee. No support team. No news reporter. Only the quiet streets of Munising greeted us.

We pulled the boat onto the shore by the city dock and let out a cheer, dancing in a few circles. Then we shook hands and cheered some more.

"We did it, Naomi. We just circumnavigated Lake Superior!"

At the pay phone, I called Dori. She said she was happy to hear we had made it back. After weeks of worry and prayers, she said she could finally rest knowing we were home safe. Dori had patiently endured the loneliness of our being apart. She marked our progress on a map as we reported back each time we could get to a phone. Now she could rest easier, knowing we were home.

Dori said she would be leaving early for her job. So I told her I would catch up with her after work. She called Caleb. He came to pick us up. Naomi and I had plenty of time to recover after the trip and get ready for the anniversary celebration. At the dinner, Naomi and I sang *Perhaps Love*, a song by John Denver. We felt good to be back with family and friends. But a part of our hearts was still out there somewhere and always will be; out there on the greatest lake in the world: Superior.

SUPERIOR'S SONG
By Carl Behrend

When I first sailed her waters
In my birch bark canoes
We fished in her rivers
We hunted on her shores
But many a brave warrior
Was taken down by her
Beneath her cold blue waters
Never to return

But I loved her then
She called me back again
Oh I loved her then

Then I sailed her waters
In my ships of wind and sail
To carry away her treasures
And live to tell the tale
But many a proud sailing ship
Was taken down by her
And many a fine sailor
Was never to return

But I loved her then
She called me back again
She said come and be my lover
Come and sail my seas
Come and take my treasures
But my lovers never leave
My lovers never leave

Then I built my lighthouses
To shine along her shore
Whitefish Point would be the first
There'd follow many more
AuSable Point and Iroquois
Grand Island and Crisp Point
All along the Shipwreck Coast
Still many ships were lost

But I loved her then
She called me back again
Oh I loved her then

I'll build my ships much stronger
I'll build my ships of steel
I'll build them with more power
Her winds I will not feel
But she took those ships to the bottom
She took those ships of steel
Took them as her lovers
Never to return

But I loved her then
She called me back again
Oh I loved her then

Then I sent my lifesavers
To rescue them from her
And the brave coast guardsmen
Stationed on her shore

Many of her lovers
Were taken away from her
Stolen by their courage
Never to return

But I loved her then
She called me back again
Oh I loved her then

Now I build my giant ships
For hauling iron ore
Ships so large and mighty
To weather any storm
Yet still she seeks her lovers
Yet still she sends her waves
For I could not tame her
But I love her just the same
And I love her still
Oh I always will
Oh I love her still

Bibliography

Boyer, Dwight. *Strange Adventures of the Great Lakes.* Dodd, Mead & Company: 1974.

Graham, Loren R. *A Face in the Rock: The Tale of the Grand Island Chippewa.* Shearwater Books (Island Press): 1995.

Keller, James M. *The Unholy Apostles.* Sheridan Books, Chelsea MI: 1984.

MacDonald, Bill, editor. *Further Emanations of Silver Islet Volume II.* Porphry Press: 1995.

Stonehouse, Frederick. *Lake Superior: Shipwreck Coast.* Avery Color Studios: 1985.

Stonehouse, Frederick. *Wreck Ashore: The United states Life Saving Service on the Great Lakes.* Lake Superior Port Cities, Inc.: 1994

Wolff, Julius F., Jr. *Lake Superior Shipwrecks.* Lake Superior Port Cities, Inc.: 1990.